COSPLAY
AND THE DRESSING
OF IDENTITY

COSPLAY

AND THE DRESSING
OF IDENTITY

Vivian Asimos

REAKTION BOOKS

To all cosplayers, and others who find themselves
in being not themselves

Published by
REAKTION BOOKS LTD
Unit 32, Waterside
44–48 Wharf Road
London N1 7UX, UK
www.reaktionbooks.co.uk

First published 2024
Copyright © Vivian Asimos 2024

Printed and bound in Great Britain
by Bell & Bain, Glasgow

A catalogue record for this book is available from the British Library

ISBN 978 1 78914 929 6

CONTENTS

Introduction:
What is Cosplay?

There are only a few magical places on this earth where, for a wonderful time, fiction comes alive. It walks among us through rows of vendors and dances for us across a stage. It takes beautiful images we cherish and love and enjoy. In this special moment, our characters – the ones we love to watch or play or read about – are suddenly walking with us, posing for photos with us, and performing their most beloved moves and sayings for us.

This is cosplay, when individuals dress as characters we love and walk with us, most often at fan conventions like Comic Con. Cosplayers are people who enjoy the simple art of dressing up, but in a way that is so much more than just dressing up.

The word 'cosplay' was first coined by game designer Nobuyoki Takahashi after encountering it at a fan convention in the United States in the 1980s. His description of this experience encouraged fans in Japan to do the same. But cosplay is more than its relationship with Japanese fiction, and it's also a lot more than just the fun art of dressing up, while always being so amazingly fun. The portmanteau of 'costume' and 'play' always has play embedded at the heart of it.

This book is going to explore the world of cosplay, and to show that it's a far more complex phenomenon than it seems on the surface. While initially it may appear to be adults taking the liberty of dressing up for Halloween a little too far, it is actually a complicated experience which helps cosplayers cope with their own lives and realities far more easily than they otherwise would.

First and foremost, I am an anthropologist. Anthropology, at its most basic, is a study of people. I study social and cultural anthropology, which means I look into how people's social and cultural worlds are built around them and affect them. As an anthropologist, I see everything we do as cultural artefacts that I can dig up and dig around like some kind of social archaeologist. My research into and around popular culture is an important part of this. I come from the understanding that popular culture represents contemporary myths, folklore and legends which reflect the ways we think, feel and act.

Anthropologists can be annoying. Our primary method of research is poking and prodding people until they decide they don't want to speak to us anymore. We ask endless questions about every aspect of human existence – we try to revert back to infancy in a way, to point at anything that appears to be basic and simple and ask 'what' and 'why' until everyone we speak to is sick of us. Anthropology, at its heart, is a collection of questions about simple things in life: why we wear what we wear when we wear it; what we say, when we say it, how we say it and to whom. We ask questions with little apparent end in sight – always anchoring them to something we can see or hear from the community itself. We go into a community like children who are eager to learn everything we can about how life is structured and why it's structured that way.

For many anthropologists, their field sites are remote locations deep in jungles where few have gone before. They travel with a voice recorder and a journal, wield a machete, and trek into the wilderness to report back on groups of people so unlike them that it's like an adventure to an alien landscape.

I, on the other hand, have my own field sites. I don't go with a machete, but with a laptop and an Internet connection. I travel not to remote villages, but to massive convention halls. I believe there is a lot to learn from every community, not just the ones in remote locations around the world. There is something fundamentally interesting about people, and this does not change with nerdy fans dressed as their favourite characters.

For my cosplay research, I did what's called 'participant observation'. This means I went to fan conventions and talked to cosplayers and watched them move through their space. I attended masquerades and cosplay competitions, and read cosplay journals. This was to observe people. I also participated by doing my own cosplay, picking a character I loved and trying to embody it as best I could. The combination of the two means I not only hear what others are saying and thinking, but know how it feels to be a cosplayer as bodily and personally as possible. Most importantly, I asked questions. I talked to cosplayers and heard their stories. I listened to what they had to say. I asked questions until they were tired of me – though most weren't. I spoke to some for five hours and still had more to think about when I left.

Some of the stories in this book are my own, through my experience in costume and participating with the community. But most are not. This is a compilation of cosplayers and their experiences. I spoke to cosplayers in both the United Kingdom and the United States. I talked to cosplayers of different races, different genders, different sexual orientations. I spoke to cosplayers of different body types and bodily abilities. Their names have been anonymized, but their words are their own. And I asked them many questions, exploring so many facets of their cosplay life, and their non-cosplay life, in order to uncover the wonderfully complicated world of cosplay.

Cosplay is often defined as dressing as fictional characters. However, this is distinguished, most of the time, from dressing up for other reasons like Halloween. It's also differentiated by many cosplayers from other forms of what I like to call 'dress play', such as histor-ical re-enactment, drag and live action role-playing (LARPing). So, what is cosplay?

When I first conceived this project, I thought it would be fairly easy to define. But I think that was my 'insider' voice talking more than my 'scholarly' voice. In anthropology, we have two terms to help differentiate these spheres: the emic (which is the under-standing from inside the object of study) and the etic (which is the understanding from outside the object of study). My initial views on cosplay were definitely influenced by my emic voice – not that I was a cosplayer myself, but I was always living around them, delving into the nerdy worlds they shared alongside me. Listening to your emic voice is not necessarily a bad thing, but it needs to be recognized, in the same way that listening to the etic voice also should be balanced.

When I allowed myself to be confused and complicated by the field, I started to see how the subject can get a little weird. When it comes to 'costume play', there are quite a few different options, from cosplay to historical re-enactors, to nerdlesque performers (burlesque routines performed in the costume of a character), to drag and even to Halloween. So how do I define these terms, both emically and etically?

The first way we can differentiate is in terms of place. Cosplay has always been associated with fan conventions like Comic Con – the art of dressing up as a figure important to that convention in order to show your deep connection to the group dynamic of fans present. When delineating by place, cosplay is easily separated from other forms of dress play because of its presence at the con. But cosplay is far more than just the con. Cosplayers take photos of their cosplays and share them online. Some even talked about cosplaying just around their hometowns, going to coffee shops with their friends all in costume.

We could look at the actual act of the various dress plays. Cosplay could be considered dressing as a fictional character, which would help to distinguish it from historical re-enactment. But some people do cosplay as non-fictional people. One talked about their first cosplays being of famous DJs. I've also seen many cosplays of YouTubers or video game streamers. At MCM London in 2023, I saw a cosplay of Taylor Swift from her '22' music video. Other forms of dress play can also include fictional characters. Historical re-enactors can make up their own character who could have lived in the time they are performing. Drag is a costumed construction of an original fictional character.

So, how do we draw these definitional boundaries? How do I – and those following and reading this like yourself – understand where cosplay exists? One thing we can do is look at how other people have drawn the boundaries. I'm not the first academic to look at cosplay – there have been others, especially from fields outside anthropology. This would require us to look at definitions and boundaries drawn by the etic voice, the scholarship which exists outside of cosplay, which is mostly what academics tend to do. In any conversation about a word or a definition, academics start by waxing on and on about what other people have said. How have others defined the field, defined the term, defined the locations? We focus on these things, and we either choose one or use existing definitions to create a new one which we hope will become one of those ideas and terms and citations in someone else's bit of waxing on and on about definitions.

But I'm going to suggest a different way. This is not inherently new in research more generally, but one which may be in our everyday lives. We focus on what people just living their lives have to say about themselves. What this means is we allow others to define themselves and where they see their own field's boundaries, and we abide by that. And, interestingly, when we allow others to show us what they think cosplay is, we also see debates between cosplayers. Maybe some think cosplays that involve revealing clothing aren't 'real' cosplay, for example. Or perhaps the way one does cosplay – such as making your own costumes – is the key, which may rub other people, such as those who buy their costumes, the wrong way.

If I had drawn my own boundaries first, like saying it requires people to make costumes or you have to perform the characters as accurately as possible, then I would be ignoring many of these fascinating debates and different viewpoints. I would be ignoring transformational cosplays, or people who bought costumes, who all define themselves as cosplayers and have their own way of looking at it.

By, instead, seeing a cosplayer as simply someone who defines themself *as a cosplayer*, I allow my definition to be fluid.

Definitions, in my opinion, need to be fluid because people are not static unmoving forces. We change and develop over our lives, and alongside major historical changes as well. Possibly, if I had been doing this same research in the 1990s, the importance of place would be far more relevant, for example. But now that cosplay has shifted to incorporate new locations and new types of cosplay, such as online, then so, too, has our understanding of what is important for cosplay to exist.

So, let us state the question again, but this time to the cosplayers who spoke to me: what is cosplay? For Arthur, it is a performance, somewhat akin to drag but distinguished by the fact that you are performing not your own character but someone else's. For Adrian, it's simply putting on a fun outfit and having a good time. For Sam, cosplay is defined by bringing a character to life. For Charlie, 'play' is paramount – a performative, playful act that combines the performer with the costume. For Riley, it's all about the connection to be had with a creative community. For Elliot, cosplay is an escape, a way of being oneself free from the typical social restraints put on adults and their inability to play.

Cosplay is different depending on who you ask, defined along different boundaries. Different aspects of cosplay are given importance in different arenas, depending on the cosplayer's own experiences. Each of these views is just as important as the previous one – even when they are so diverse – because cosplay is complicated and beautiful and intricate. And we're going to uncover every bit of it.

1

Myth, Pop Culture and Cosplay

I will always remember the first time I truly understood the ending of *The Lord of the Rings*. I know it's popular to tease about the multiple endings, the way you think the movie ends and then you see another hour of content – or, in the case of the books, another two hundred or so pages. And I get that, for sure. I'm not a huge fan of movies, so you would think one that drags on an extra hour for no real reason would not exactly make me happy.

But then I experienced my own post-traumatic stress. And suddenly, seeing those hobbits sitting uncomfortably back in Hobbiton, not knowing how to even hold themselves in the pub where they once felt the most themselves – it really made sense. I was those hobbits. I realized, then, that this was the first time a piece of fantasy had told me there was no happily ever after where the world returned to normal and everyone was peaceful and con-tent for the rest of their days. No. Merry and Pippin were so unable to settle that they returned to being soldiers for Gondor and Rohan. Frodo essentially killed himself by retiring to the lands with the elves across the sea. Life was hard for them on return. It taught me that, sometimes, there's no returning to the peace you felt before. And surprisingly, there was comfort in that.

I am not alone in seeing myself in stories. In fact, that's often how we find ourselves. It's how we make connections with those around us and form our communities, through the stories we tell about ourselves and about others. It's how we define the boundaries of these communities – what makes us different from them. I want to start our exploration of cosplay through a discussion of story, and more importantly a form of story we often refer to as 'mythology'.

When I was growing up, my mother had a few stories she repeated a lot. Like most mothers, it didn't matter if I told her I already knew the story – she was going to complete it as if it was my first time hearing it. Every time. A favourite of hers was of two Buddhist monks walking through a forest. At a river, they encountered a woman who needed help to cross. One of the monks picked up the woman and carried her across the river – even though touching women was forbidden. As they continued their walk, the other monk kept thinking about the transgression his companion had made, until finally he broke and demanded his friend explain why he would do such a thing. His friend said, 'I put the woman down on the other side of the river. How long have you been carrying her?'

For some, in order for any story, including ones like my mother's Zen stories, it must have certain narrative elements to be considered mythology. And here, I want to try not to wax on about definitions as I said academics tend to do. Narrative element-based definitions are what scholars call 'substantialist' definitions. They include elements of a story like how the narrative must be about gods, for example. But there are lots of cultures around the world

– and the Zen stories would fall into this category – which do not have gods. These substantialist definitions also require people looking and studying myths to decide which elements are considered significant and which are not – typically from a standpoint outside the culture they are studying. Often, these elements are chosen from white Christian cultures, meaning elements – such as gods – are only considered important to include because they are important for the cultures the scholars are coming from. But they may not be important for the cultures being looked at.

Instead, others think of myths as an explanation for the world – why lightning exists and what exactly it is, for example; it's Thor who gives us lightning. Or maybe it is why spiders exist, through Athena being mad at Arachne's ability to weave. But what about narratives like my mother's about the monks? In this story, there are no explanations of how things have come to this world or why natural occurrences are present. Stories like *The Iliad* or *The Odyssey* do not carry inherent explanations for the natural order of the world in them either.

E. B. Tylor was a scholar who understood myth as explanation. The idea was that ancient peoples needed to have some kind of rational explanation for the natural occurrences around them. Today we have science to explain these things, but before humans had science, they needed something else. So, they had myths.[1]

This is a simplistic understanding of both the power of storytelling as well as the minds of ancient peoples. Humans have always had the conception of rational thought, even if they lacked ways of seeing tiny molecules. This also does not provide a good explanation for other types of stories, such as myths focusing on a hero's exploits (such as Odysseus, for example) or even more ideologically focused narratives like my mother's Zen stories.

Folklorist William Bascom has a solution. For him, what set a myth apart from other forms of narrative was that myths were considered to be 'truthful' accounts of what happened in the past.[2] Following his lead, many others began setting narratives into two camps: those considered fictional and those considered factual.

Then there are my mother's Zen monks. Another story she used to tell me was of a monk walking through the woods and coming across a rabbit. A little later, a hunter runs up to the monk and asks if the monk saw which way the rabbit went. The monk asks why, and the hunter explains, 'I'm a hunter – I need to kill the rabbit to eat.' Now, according to Zen Buddhism, one is not meant to cause harm to others. If the monk tells the hunter which way the rabbit went, he causes harm to the rabbit. But if he doesn't, he's causing harm to the hunter.

And to my childish dismay, that's where the story ends. I never knew which way the hunter chose because that's not the point of the story. The monk didn't factually exist at some point in the past. This dilemma he was faced with didn't actually occur. Its reality, or fictionality, was not why the story was told in the first place. For my mother, the historical existence of these various monks is not important, nor is it even really considered. They live for the narrative that the story imparts. We also see this spring up in some considerations of Christian mythology (though not for all branches of Christianity, of course). For some, the myths found in Genesis of the origin of humans and the fall from Eden are not historically accurate but are still important.

So, there are all sorts of different types of truth here when we are talking about mythology. For Tylor and those like him, myths tell a scientific 'truth', for Bascom a historical truth. My mother's stories don't fit either of these truths. She never considered the existence of these stories as historically true or as scientific truths in any form – they don't provide explanations for natural phenomena. She knew these stories would fall into the category Bascom labelled as 'fiction', and yet she told them to me in a way that was important. The meaningfulness of her narratives was not tied to some grand historical grounding.

But they also weren't 'sacred' in the way people in the United Kingdom or United States may think of the word – another word often related to the idea of myths. My mother did not think of these stories as set apart from the everyday, as special and elevated and more than normal. They were not about gods either, or sacred realms in a place and time before time. These were narratives spoken in the heart of everyday life, often when I did not want to hear them, as part of our normal conversation and communication as mother and daughter. They were as important as family dinners, or as sacred as a mother's attempt to keep her daughter from harm. Any scholar studying this interaction of storytelling would see nothing in the performance or the telling of the story as being any different from lightly chatting with me about how school was or telling me I can't wear a skirt that short. That is not to say my mother's stories are unimportant, but rather they demonstrate the utmost importance of the everyday experience. Storytelling is not necessarily as simple and straightforward to explain and define as 'important' or 'not important', or as 'true' and 'not true'.

Some might consider this a type of metaphor.[3] Metaphors relate two things together in a way that seems to combine them. When I'm gossiping with a friend, and my friend says 'that girl is a snake,' I don't think my friend mistakenly believes that girl is a reptile, but rather she can't be trusted. The idea is that myths work in the same way – these stories are not saying that this stuff literally happened, but rather they are stand-ins for something else, like who can or cannot be trusted.

But there is a problem with this approach, too. This assumes a particular ideological 'proper' stance – basically, some things are going to be considered as possible while others are not and are therefore clearly metaphor. It's impossible the girl my friend is referring to is an actual snake, and therefore I know to read it as a metaphor. But some cultures and worldviews hold conceptions of reality we may think of as impossible. This does not mean one worldview is inherently wrong or flawed, only that it's different. To assume, for example, that a story of rocks moving is a metaphor may discount the cultures who believe rocks can, in fact, move. Not because they are rocks – or that people from these cultures are wrong – but because these specific rocks are people, and people can move with agency.

So myth is not a metaphor, and it's not an overt lie, and it's not a stand-in for scientific truth, nor is it a sacred truth. For me, and for this book going forward, we are going to understand myth as this: a meaningful narrative, or something like a narrative, which an individual or a community uses to understand themselves and the world around them.[4]

For my mother, the point of her stories was to help me understand the world and my place within it. I was taught that the world would present me with situations in which I would have to choose between two bad options (the monk and the hunter). I was taught that it is worse to hold on to past grievances than to just let them go (the two monks and the woman). These were important instructions a mother felt necessary to pass on to her daughter. I needed to be prepared – to know myself and the way the world would treat me. Another very Buddhist-like saying of my mother's was 'life sucks and then you die' – a short, pithy way to understand how the world would treat me when I was an adult. These are not sacred truths, they're not set apart from the world. In fact, they're inherently part of it; they are the communication of entirely profane truths, a fundamental explanation of the everyday. They revealed the basic functioning of the mundane realities I would face. They were banal truths, inherently immensely important truths, based entirely in fiction.

Okay, so we've seen how mythology has a complicated relationship with fiction. But I'm sure it's easy to see how myth can also be fiction when its stories are of legendary heroes or Buddhist monks. What about stories from Middle-earth or heroes from Hyrule? For many, it's okay to say fictional stories relating to religion or ideology are acceptable for mythology, but not stories played out in video games or on our television screens. But we have to think about the differences in storytelling between previous times and contemporary times. What makes something like my mother's Zen monks somehow more magical – or mythic – than, say, *Game of Thrones*?

Perhaps time is a big factor. Old Zen stories or the saga of Odysseus or legends of Thor are all very old narratives. We think of them as having a legacy, a history which reaches far back. This history is what gives them legitimization as 'sacred' narratives – they are important simply because they continue to exist. And there is something interesting there. Many stories, even contemporary popular culture narratives, have fallen from view while others have stuck around. The staying power of certain narratives is interesting – what makes them more important or more interesting for audiences than whatever new narrative comes around?

That being said, 'old' is not a prerequisite for 'important'. At one point in time, the story of the Zen monks was a new tale, one newly heard by new adherents to some new religion which sprang up as an offshoot of an older tradition. At one point in time, Buddhism was new in Japan, and the traditions of Japanese Zen Buddhism were just starting. These narratives helped to give space to the new worldview in its infancy, a demonstration of how these adherents who had finally found something to understand their place in the world understood themselves. And when these stories were new, they were not less important to the people who told them than they were to my mother, reciting these old tales she had heard time and time again to her daughter, who had also heard them so many times before.

Back when I was teaching religion at Durham University, I found the idea of 'old' being equated with 'importance' a hefty idea to break in new students. What I always enjoyed pointing out was that the long-lasting tradition of Christianity, which many of them were adherents of, was at one point new. And at that time, these narratives we all recognize, and the way this worldview understood itself, were new as well.

Our earlier definition of myth put all the significance of a narrative in the hands of people who have the choice of whether to continue to tell these stories or whether to ignore them. For those who continue to tell the stories, there's something that makes them important and appealing. For many, it connects them to their own understanding of the world. If a myth is what an individual or a community uses to understand the complicated relationship between self and world, to comprehend and make sense of our place within this world, then whether the story is new or old is of really no consequence – what's important is how people *feel* about the narrative.

In essence, mythology and mythic storytelling did not stop at some point after the Greek pantheon or the Norse gods; it has continued to live on and exist in our storytelling – it exists right now in the stories we continue to tell. It lives in the way we are excited to show our children our favourite movie when we were young. Or in how nervous we may be to share our favourite book with a love interest, fearing their rejection of it will equal a rejection of us. The way it looks, and how we encounter it, are just a little different.

Popular culture encompasses so much of our everyday lives, from what we watch to what we read, how we dress and even what we eat. There can obviously be meaning for individuals outside of what is popular or even to retain that meaning even when something is no longer as popular as it once was. But popular culture is made popular by us, by a culture or society at large, and this is of particular interest to those like me looking for meaningful narratives.

When we look into fan cultures and people who really love their bits of popular culture, we can very easily see individuals who gravitate towards narratives because they matter to them. When we grab hold of a narrative tightly, we do so because we see something within it – we see ourselves, or the world we understand or comprehend. I grabbed hold of *The Lord of the Rings* because I saw my experiences with PTSD in its pages. I understood the experience of feeling like there was no possible way of returning home for a happily ever after. My worldview, my understanding of my place in the world, had radically shifted, and I grabbed hold of the narrative that showed me the world as I now understood it to be.

When doing research into *The Legend of Zelda* games, I encountered a lot of similar sentiments in other people. One person I chatted to had a tattoo of a Triforce – an image of three triangles arranged together in a bigger triangle – on their forearm. The Triforce is an important symbol in the *Zelda* franchise. In the game world, it's an object of great sacred importance, left behind by the three goddesses who created the world. Each triangle represents an important facet of a person: wisdom, power and courage. The in-game myth is that anyone who has a perfect balance of wisdom, power and courage can touch the Triforce and have any wish they want granted. If they do not have this balance, the Triforce breaks into three separate pieces, each piece spiritually attaching itself to someone who is the embodiment of its human facet. The person who had the tattoo spoke to me about this part of the story, and said it was always so amazing how each game forced you to play out each element. Your primary character had to have a balance of wisdom, power and courage in order to successfully beat the game. They expressed to me how much this meant to them, and said the tattoo was there to help guide them through their life: to approach every decision with an equal balance of wisdom, power and courage.

Now, this lovely participant would by no means be marking the United States census record with 'Hylian' as their religion. They probably don't see their connection to this narrative as being overly sacred, or a metaphor, or a historic truth. But this narrative is an important guiding light for them; it demonstrates a way to exist and move in the world. It gives them a way to understand themselves. Playing the game was a fun experience, but it also provided them with a more nuanced understanding of the world they live in, and they continued to use the game as a narrative to better understand it. In other words, for this player, and for myself with *The Lord of the Rings*, these stories in pop culture are inherently mythic.

There is a widespread view that consumers of popular culture are somehow passive – that we wade through the world sluggish

COSPLAY AND THE DRESSING OF IDENTITY

and blind, picking up whatever corporations place in our hands. While large corporations can definitely control much of what we see around us, we have a lot of control over what we take in and what we don't. Things tend to be popular for a reason – and it's not always simple.

Even children are often not passive consumers. In the past kids' television shows were used as the primary mechanism to sell toys – the driver of profit was the toys and not the show itself. Mattel had a figure of a very muscular man with long blond hair – a surfer dude figurine they were trying to sell. And it was not selling. So Mattel hired a myth specialist to write a story for this figure, and suddenly the figure was different – he became He-Man and fronted a detailed fantastical mythology of 'Masters of the Universe'.[5] He-Man's popularity grew tremendously, even starting spin-offs aimed for young girls with She-Ra. Suddenly, it was not just a basic surfer dude toy, but a connection to a mythic narrative of 'Masters of the Universe', and an incentive for kids everywhere to lift their stand-ins for swords and shout 'by the power of Grayskull'.

The story of He-Man shows us something important. The same figure, with the same appearance, sold massively differently when there was a different story attached to it. We gravitate towards stories that mean something to us, that tell us something we need in our lives. Children before He-Man didn't care about the story of a surfer dude. But they were obsessed with the story of He-Man. If corporations could sell anything, the surfer dude would have been sufficient for our passive hands. But it wasn't. Even children saw nothing to understand about the self in the surfer story. They dropped it on purpose. But with He-Man, they grabbed it readily.

Even as children, we are discerning when it comes to what matters to us. We don't just grab something because it's in front of us, or else the surfer dude would have done well. No, we need mythic connections to our narratives – we need something meaningful. Even as children, we crave the ability to connect to narratives and invite them into our lives, but we won't take just any narrative. We want something more concrete, more meaningful. We want something mythic.

But the thing about He-Man is that this isn't just a story about mythic success, it's also one about financial success. I think this example is also the best one to demonstrate whether or not something made for the purposes of profit can still be meaningful and mythic. Obviously, Mattel did want to just make money. Their surfer figurine wasn't moving off shelves, and it was losing them profits. The company didn't change its mindset away from profit in order to make He-Man successful – money was still the sole reasoning. And yet, the result was so different.

I don't know whether we'd have He-Man if it wasn't for the ever-pressing push of the capitalist need to make money. But we don't have to change lenses from mythic to capitalist to view different sides of the He-Man story – these lenses are not as separate and different as they may appear to be. For He-Man to be successful and make the money Mattel wanted, it had to be mythic. To ignore the myth is to ignore what made him successful. And equally, to ignore his history is to also ignore an interesting part of his story.

The ever-present drive of capitalism is not what makes or breaks a narrative, but rather the people who have the choice to pick up what they like and discard what they don't. Children discarded the surfer but picked up He-Man. We do not move through our culture like drones, but rather like poachers, as Michel de Certeau described. De Certeau, writing in the 1970s as He-Man figurines flew off the shelves, showed how active some consumers are, how they do not just sit back and let pop culture happen to them. They participate actively.[6] We sit around our co-workers' desks talking about *Love Island* not because *Love Island* is forced on to us as a talking point, but because we want to talk about it. We get tattoos of the Triforce because we connect inherently to *The Legend of Zelda* video games. We voraciously read everything Tolkien provided because we see something of ourselves in *The Lord of the Rings*.

De Certeau described audiences as poachers, meaning we move in the fictional worlds we find ourselves in and take what we like.[7] His work focused more on the practice of reading, but I think it can apply to other forms of popular culture as well. In fact, Henry Jenkins took de Certeau's concept of poaching and related it to the way fans comb narratives to make them their own.[8]

Fandom was first understood as something to be avoided. Fans were the over-enthused 'other'; those strange fanatics who would love something to excess, spreading it to others and becoming so immensely emotionally attached to it, were a psychological problem. We have grown to understand fandom as healthy – there are many types of fan out there, and fans for all sorts of different things. Fans are those who find solace, in one way or another, in an everyday part of popular culture.

Cornel Sandvoss, a scholar in the academic study of fandom, defined it as 'the regular, emotionally involved consumption of a given popular narrative or text'.[9] These fans, therefore, are the clear indicators of how contemporary audiences engage with contemporary stories – with emotional connections and investments which have the potential to directly affect the audience on a deeper level. They are the ones who see the piece of popular culture as mythic.

Through fandom, we see emotional connections that influence the formation and alteration of personal identities. Through their connection to popular culture, fans grow to understand themselves and also the world around them. My participant with the Triforce tattoo is one of these – a fan of *Zelda* whose emotional attachment to the game is reflected in how they use the narrative to understand how they must move through the world.

For fans like the participant with the *Zelda* tattoo, it is more than over-enthusiasm for something that is 'just a game'. They are not psychological 'others' who need some kind of help. They are simply people who find solace in a narrative, and this solace allows them to better understand themselves and the social world they find themselves in. The fact that these narratives are more often fictional has no bearing on their ability to function as myths – just as my mother's Buddhist monks could be fictional. Humans can separate the idea of myth and fiction, seeing them as two categories which can overlap without any problem.

If we think about mythology in the sense of old stories rather than new ones, then we would have to ask an important question: when did myths stop being told? And following that: why did we ever stop? The answer, as we can see through aspects of life like fandom and popular culture narratives that are important to the people telling them, retelling them and engaging with them, is that, quite simply, they have never stopped. We never stopped telling meaningful stories. The form they take, however, has shifted a little.

Popular culture is our mythology, our contemporary narratives of heroes and gods and fantastical worlds. It communicates our world back to us, and we either grab it wholeheartedly or reject it completely. Like my participant with the *Zelda* tattoo, we mark these narratives on our skin and use them to guide us through life. Like my relationship with *Lord of the Rings*, it teaches us that our individual views of the world are not crazy – we are similar to others, and we can find a new life. Like my mother's Zen stories, they are fictional but meaningful and so important to pass down to the generations after us.

So where does cosplay fit in this world of mythological contemporary stories? While we have spent some time looking at storytelling more generally in this chapter, cosplay is the reason for this book and our focus going forward. What does cosplay show us about our contemporary mythology and its ability to create and provide meaning? I believe that to truly understand cosplay we have to first understand popular culture as mythology. Cosplay is an inherent function of this engagement with what we call pop mythology – it's the way we bring narratives to life.

If we think of the 'old' myths – the Norse gods, the Greek pantheon – we have to remember these stories were never simply written and read while killing time at a cafe, as we sometimes engage with them now. In fact, many of them were not written down until new religions and ways of thinking were being introduced to that world, as was the case for the Norse gods. The stories were brought to life through performance, the art of oral recitation or theatrical renditions. People would don masks and 'become' the mythic figure, acting out the stories through dance and bodily movement. Stories are not always read on paper. They can also be comprehended through watching, through engagement and through listening. Theatre now, for example, tells stories which the audience understands through watching. We know the narrative as fiction and meaningful, and can also remember that the actor is just an actor. But for the two hours we sit in the theatre, that actor is not an actor – they are the character and we understand them as the character.

Cosplay is a performance, one that demonstrates the performer's intense interest and connection to the narrative being performed. It is also done on behalf of others who equally love the narrative.

As part of anthropological participant-observation, my research into cosplay meant two things: I observe, but I also participate. So I cosplayed. When deciding which character to cosplay, I actually had a pretty hard time choosing. I like a lot of things. I obviously love *Lord of the Rings*, as I've already mentioned, but I also love a lot of video games like *The Legend of Zelda* and *Bastion*. I love reading fiction, and am particularly fond of *The Dresden Files*. Out of all these things I feel a connection to, how do I choose?

When cosplayers are deciding for themselves who they want to cosplay, they generally consider two factors: the cosplayer and the location the cosplay will occur in. In essence, as the cosplay performer, they have to consider themselves and how they feel about a character. They also have to consider the audience they are performing for, and the spaces they will be moving in.

For the performer side of things, the cosplayer needs a character who relates to them as an individual. This can mean a few different things, depending on the person. One participant I chatted to, for example, discussed looking for characters who have personality traits they want to embody themselves. The cosplay performance allows them to embody these traits, even if only temporarily. Some of these connections can be sought more directly, looking for a character who fully embodies aspects of themselves. Another person I spoke to told me of how they cosplayed a character who had lost their mother and remained strong. The cosplayer had also recently lost their mother and saw an intense similarity in the experience of grief.

There is a second part of the choice, however: the audience. One person told me a story about their excitement at cosplaying Shiklah, a character from the *Deadpool* comics. They thought that because *Deadpool* is a popular cosplay choice for many people, they would get a lot of recognition and interaction. Not one person recognized them. They felt dejected, and voiced regret at having made the costume in the first place, despite their excitement about it leading up to the event.

If the cosplay is for a con, like the Shiklah cosplay, the type of con and who will be there is an important consideration for the cosplayer. CosXpo is an event entirely devoted to cosplay and cosplay alone in the United Kingdom. While there, one participant told me they enjoyed how at CosXpo they could cosplay more obscure characters, because the primary interest was in the costume quality and details rather than on recognition of character. In contrast, at something like a Comic Con, they felt more pressure to do a character a wider array of people would like because attendees want to see their favourite characters.

Cosplays can also be done purely for the Internet and not for a con. Many cosplayers will do photoshoots of their cosplays and put them online through social media platforms like Instagram. In this case, wider recognition may be less important, as you can tag specific groups to get niche audiences to see it, but attention to modelling and how the costume comes across in a photograph is more important.

These two parts of the performance choice – the cosplayer and the audience – take a detailed understanding and connection to

Myself, Vivian Asimos, as Chise Hatori from *The Ancient Magus' Bride*.

the stories chosen. When it comes to the cosplayer, the connection to narrative is more obvious – the cosplayer is actively choosing characters based entirely on their emotional attachment to the narrative. In other words, cosplayers are choosing their character based on their view of the narrative as more mythic. For the audience, understanding the narrative's connection to broader communities, and therefore the performer's understanding of these communities, is what is needed.

For my cosplay, I thought about the many characters I loved but also about my own body and abilities. I chose to cosplay Chise Hatori from the Japanese anime *The Ancient Magus' Bride*. I chose Chise for several reasons: the first is that *The Ancient Magus' Bride* is one of my favourite anime, and the second is that the outfit choice would be easy to replicate and would make me feel comfortable. But there is also a third reason. As someone who has struggled with anxiety and depression, I saw myself and my own experiences in the depression of Chise. I'm personally uncomfortable with my body being dressed immodestly, and felt I would be most comfortable moving around at cons and in photographs when not as concerned about the display of my body. One of the things I did not pay as much attention to is the role of audience. I only started to realize the importance of the audience after cosplaying at conventions, but we'll discuss that further in a later chapter.

In both parts of the process of deciding what to cosplay, the connection the individual has to pop mythology is demonstrated. Both aspects of the character choice feed into the ultimate conception of pop culture as an integral part of meaning-making for the communities and the individual, while also relying on the cosplayer to embody the narrative in such a convincing way as to allow the story to continue to live in new environments. Like the storyteller performers of old, cosplayers can tell stories with their own spin on them, such as gender transformations or fusion characters.

All this focus on meaning can make it sound like cosplay is stressful and burdensome. But fun is at root of it. Something can be both meaningful and fun at the same time – this is what pop mythology is all about. The whole point of cosplay is that it offers a great sense of fun and entertainment for both the cosplayer and their audience.

Cosplay is an inherently meaningful experience, mostly because it arises from popular culture, which we connect to through our understanding of and love for the stories surrounding us. Popular culture is our contemporary mythology not because it points to a mystic history or because it explains the science of the world, but because it reflects human experience. We see ourselves in the stories, and we see our own way of understanding the world we move through. Cosplayers embody these narratives. They cosplay through their own connections to community and narrative, and feel more connected to the story through their costumes. The cosplayer's performance lives out the narrative and connects them to the story through their body and their costume.

The costume is incredibly important. Despite there being various definitions of cosplay, we can all agree that to some extent costumes are involved. Dressing – and dress plays more generally – unveil interesting dynamics to the intersections of dress, performance and narrative. The definition of myth I proposed in this chapter is a narrative, or something akin to a narrative, that an individual or community uses to understand themselves and the world around them. There is a reason why I added that 'something akin to a narrative' part. We sometimes think of narratives as words that are either spoken or written down, but we can tell stories in other ways. The art of dressing tells a story. Our clothes, therefore, can be stories which communicate identities and narratives of ourselves – or, in the case of cosplayers, other people as whom we are performing.

2

The Art of Dressing

Many would say the art of cosplay began in the 1980s and '90s with the rise of mainstream mass pop culture media and the growth of fan conventions and comic cons. While this was when the term 'cosplay' was coined, there has been a long history of people dressing up as fictional characters. We could, of course, begin by drawing connections to traditional dances and performances of mythical characters and stories, though for now I will put that aside. Even without this influence, similar circumstances of ceremonial and artful dressing of characters can be traced to the Carnival of Venice, whose many stock characters and masks create an environment for individuals to feel more like themselves in society.

Obviously, the history of cosplay is also dependent on its definition. When thinking about the history of dressing in special outfits, we would have to consider the extensive background of folk costumes. But if we stick to the typical understanding of cosplay as dressing as a fictional character for a particular event of common interest, we also see this reaching far earlier than the 1980s. In March 1877, Jules Verne hosted his first masked ball, where attendees dressed as characters from his books.[1] Masquerades in general were sometimes used as opportunities for attendees to dress as

Wins First Prize As "Skygack"

Times readers don't need to ask who the dickens this is. Sure, it's Skygack from Mars, one of the Times' humorous characters. August Olson of Monroe, Wash., contributed the picture. He "made up" as Skygack and "copped" the first prize at a masked ball at Monroe.

August Olson as Mr Skygack, from *Tacoma Times*, 24 May 1912.

characters from literature, literally masking their own identity in their outfits. In 1912 August Olson dressed as Mr Skygack, a comic strip character, at a masquerade. Even in terms of fan conventions, the history is longer than one may think. The first cosplayer is often thought of as being Myrtle R. Douglas, who cosplayed alongside her then boyfriend Forrest Ackerman at Worldcon in 1939.[2]

The history of cosplay is long and complicated because the exact nature of cosplay, as opposed to other forms of dressing up, is also rather difficult to untangle. Cosplay has a lot of similarities with other forms of what I like to call 'dress play': activities where individuals dress with the purpose of playing around with identity. Drag, live action role-play and historical re-enactment are just three examples of different forms of dress play which have intersecting moments with cosplay. In fact, many cosplayers often interact with these other forms of dress play, sometimes without really thinking about the boundary lines between one and the other. During one of my interviews, a cosplayer talked to me openly about what they viewed as the difference between drag and cosplay, and pointed out how some people will cosplay as other people's 'dragsonas', or drag characters. When cosplaying as drag, these are not drag performers but cosplayers, and are viewed as just that. So people can cosplay real people, fake people and fake people portrayed exclusively by real people. And all the while, they are dipping in and out of different definitions of what cosplay both is and has the potential to be.

People can't be perfectly situated in labelled boxes. What we'd like to be a clean and tidy closet is more like a complete mess someone gave up halfway through organizing. People cannot be neatly folded into one box, but rather they lounge across multiple boxes, intimately tied up around others in a complicated heap of tangled labels. That's not to say labels and definitions are not useful. The person is lounging across multiple boxes, but not *every* box. I'll take my wins where I can. Most cosplayers are tangled scarves lounging across the boxes of 'scarves', 'winter gear' and 'accessories'. While I attempt to untangle some aspects, I think one of the things that makes cosplayers – and people in general – so interesting is the inability to neatly categorize at all.

The reasons why drag, LARP, re-enactment and other forms of dress play are so complicated is because dressing is such an important part of our lives as social beings. A lot of studies of fashion and dress talk about how fashion is a form of communication. As fashion scholar Malcolm Barnard puts it, fashion is what makes 'us' into 'us'.[3] It becomes a form of identity creation and cohesion, and allows people who are 'us' to recognize 'us', while also making it very clear to 'them' that they are not 'us'.

People have been using dress in this way for a very long time. Religious dress is often the marker of the in-group versus out-group, as well as a way of communicating beliefs and worldviews. The hijab, for example, is not only a marker of Muslim identity, but carries with it the implicit and multifaceted meanings behind the hijab and the reason for its wearing in the first place. We seldom wear something just to wear it. Even clothing such as modest dress is a way to mark morality and belief on the body, and separate the self from others who may be different.

There are all sorts of terms to give to the clothes we wear: fashion, garb, dress, clothing. From an everyday standpoint, these terms feel interchangeable, synonyms to swap in and out whenever it seems appropriate. But like most things, anthropologically there are a lot of different definitions and ideas tied to these various words. Some, however, do impact the everyday understanding of the words. Saying 'clothing', for example, sounds very mundane and typical, while 'fashion' carries a sense of grandeur and glamour. I'll typically be using the words 'dress' and 'dressing' to talk about clothing and the process of putting clothes on a body for one specific reason: anthropology has a long history of talking about dress and adornment, and in the discipline it is used as a more all-inclusive term to talk about the variety of things people do to their body.[4]

When we get dressed, it is not just the clothes we must consider. Clothes go on to a body. It is through our bodies that we see, and are seen by, the world. Seeing me is also seeing my body and seeing the dressing on my body. Anthropologist Mary Douglas wrote about how we all have two bodies: a physical one and a social one. The social body in many ways controls the way our physical bodies are read and understood by the people around us.

Our physical experiences and understanding of our physical body are always 'clothed' by our social categories and social worlds. In many ways, there is no such thing as a nude body, because we are always clothed in these thoughts and considerations. Douglas's two bodies are always in interaction and communication with each other, constantly reinforcing the categories of one on to the other.[5] Essentially, our bodies are more than biological mechanisms. They are also social tools for communication and categorization. For example, my gender is inscribed as both a social body and a physical body, and which gender I am is read through the social and used as a way to believe an understanding about the physical.

Dressing and fashion are always located in the world in a physical sense. They have a locality, a spatiality, a physical presence that takes up space in the world. Maurice Merleau-Ponty, a French philosopher, pointed out how our body 'inhabits or haunts space'. Essentially, bodies are always taking up space. Our experiences with our bodies come from the movements we make around the world.[6]

The fact that our dressed bodies inhabit the world around us – spatially, temporally – is important because when we get dressed, we do so with knowledge of the world we inhabit. We always orient our dressing to the places and spaces we are in and going to. When I was teaching at a university, I would dress for my classes differently than if I was going on a date with my husband. We also dress for the larger social worlds we are in. As a woman with a feminine body, I have to be incredibly aware of the way my society views my body, and dress accordingly. Even for those who fight against these social constraints put upon a gendered or social body, you are still in some way taking them into consideration. Purposefully dressing counter to social expectation requires understanding the social expectation.

But our bodies, and our dressed bodies, are not just for the social worlds around us. Sociologist Erving Goffman pointed out how the body is not just a property of the social world, but property of the individual.[7] In fact, our bodies are the way we explain and demonstrate our identities to the people around us. Clothes provide us with the ingredients necessary to perform our identities. Fashion scholar Fred Davis explains how our dress provides a 'a kind of visual metaphor for identity'.[8]

This is important to remember, because as much as the social worlds around us have expectations and ways of reading our bodies, this is not done without our own impact. People can try and subvert expectations directly by purposefully dressing in a way that denies the expectation. Gender, and the way gender dynamics play on dressing and fashion, is a good example of this. There are certain conventions expected of a particularly gendered body that relate to fashion: in the United States and United Kingdom, for example, dresses were reserved for women, while trousers were reserved for men. Historically, women fought to wear trousers by just wearing them, subverting the expectation and changing the social restrictions on the female gendered body by directly playing against them. In more recent fashion news, the move for male-gendered celebrities to wear skirts and dresses at important events, such as Harry Styles and Billy Porter, works to subvert expectations of gender and the gender binary put upon bodies. These examples demonstrate how individuals have agency over their bodies and the way their physical bodies are dressed, despite gendered power dynamics working on their social body. By dressing their physical body in a specific way, they are directly altering the perceptions put upon the physical by the social, while also acknowledging and having full knowledge of the existence of these perceptions.

Clothes and dressing are a form of communicating ourselves to the world around us. We demonstrate our interests, our community groups and our morals through the way we dress. There's a lot of research available on the way subcultures dress to express their identity.[9] Punk, for example, utilized fashion to directly cause comment in mainstream society. But subcultural style is just one example of the many ways we dress to denote our identities, morals and social connections.

I tend to dress quite modestly. This is not because I think all women should, but because my relationship to my social body and the reading of the gendered body I have make me more inclined not to fight the social reading, and rather try to avoid it entirely. I know, rationally, this is not how it works, but I am more comfortable in more modest clothing because I'm not actively worried about the social reading of other people as much as when I'm less covered. This modest way of dressing is a way of communicating my identity. I am not the type of person to be loud and argue against society in upfront ways like punk subcultural style does. In many ways, the choice to dress modestly demonstrates a lot about how I approach the social world more generally. I don't actively fight against the ways society views my body, which shows how I dislike direct confrontation.

When we talk about our dress reflecting our personality and interests, this can be in obvious ways, like subcultural styles or the wearing of band T-shirts. Or it can be more subtle, like modest fashion or floral prints. Cosplay demonstrates an intricate knowledge of how dress and the dressed body impact the way people communicate their identities, whether implicitly or explicitly. By studying outfits, cosplayers are able to understand which aspects of costumes are important for communicating and performing the identity of the individual they are cosplaying.

Many of the people I spoke to explained how they negotiate creating a costume by determining which elements were the most important to maintain from the fictional character, which elements to change and which to completely remove. Bailey, for example, talked about not bothering to make certain layers of a costume if they weren't necessary for character recognition.

Cosplay also reveals the intricate relationship between body and dressing. Many participants have expressed a change in their confidence when cosplaying, even when outside of cosplay. Grayson, for example, told me that 'cosplay's about being, like, giving that extra boost of confidence as well.' In fact, the confidence gained through cosplaying was Grayson's favourite and most notable part of it. 'For me, particularly, it would be the confidence . . . in body. Confidence. Because I feel like I'm more confident as that character. I feel more pretty as that character. I feel more . . . I feel like I'm more accepted as that character than I am myself.' The art of dressing, and the performance associated with it, have an impact not only on the performance but on the body which did the dressing. You can't really talk about dress without talking about the body, and the way dressing impacts the body and the body impacts the dressing. Cosplayers will, for example, transform a costume to have a head covering for people who culturally wear a head covering, or use either wigs or natural hair for Black cosplayers even when the original character does not have that type of hair. In these instances, the body of the cosplayer is also impacting the way the dressing happens. Cosplay is ultimately an activity which incorporates elements of the body, the art of dressing, and the performance associated with the body and dress.

So clothing tells a story, whether it's clothing on a fictional character or clothing on a physical person in front of us. When we're talking about the role of mythology and storytelling in cosplay, the way one dresses and the fact that dressing itself is a way of telling a story are incredibly important.

We tell a story about ourselves when we dress, which means we also read information about a person when we look at them in dress. When artists, writers and other creators craft characters, they consider these elements. How does the character dress, and what does that mean for the character and what we, as an audience, should think about the character? Therefore, when cosplayers are looking at costumes to replicate, they are, in essence, also thinking about the character's identity in relation to the dress.

The ability of costumes and dressing to tell a story is also understood by some folklore scholars. There is a subset of folklore studies focusing on other forms of storytelling than traditional words. Bodylore, as it's called, refers to the way the body has its own text, where culture and tradition are received, understood and transmitted.[10] We do very little without our bodies, including the way we tell and understand stories. Bodylore highlights some of what we've already talked about: how the body is central to communication and identity, and is the central form through which we engage and interact with the social worlds around us. What bodylore centrally understands is that the body is inherently performative and is the way in which we transmit and communicate our identity to people around us, through these performances.[11]

When a cosplayer inhabits the identity of the dress of the character, their body is still the cosplayer's. This means there is a complicated double relationship of communication happening with cosplayers – not only are they performing the identity of the character, but they are performing the identity of themselves. The cosplayer's body is still there, and still communicating certain relationships these types of bodies have with the social worlds around them; the body's abilities or disabilities, skin colour and gender all impact the way the social world understands them, even when in cosplay. But the character's identity is tied in with this communication.

This means there are two ways cosplayers can understand their own body's relationship to the original media to create a new text in their representation: the first is in direct imitation, where they endeavour to maintain 'accuracy' to the original, including costumes, performances and the body; and the second is in textual transformation, where the cosplayer takes advantage of the differences between the original text and themself to adapt it.[12] Of course, these aren't exclusive categories. Cosplayers can fall into both types depending on the cosplay they are doing, as well as delving into and out of these categories depending on the act they are doing. They may seek to be more like direct imitation when taking photos, but happy to be adaptive when at cons, for example.

Storytelling and mythology in relation to performances and actions of the body call up questions of ritual, and the connection ritual may or may not have with cosplay. In the previous chapter, we already discussed how mythology was not, historically, simply read or spoken. Myths were performed, sometimes with masks and outfits, around a fire or on a stage. Cosplay is a donning of masks and outfits, and sometimes involves a performance of story with the body and the voice.

The differences between ritual and habit is a discussion in ritual studies and other anthropological approaches to ritual that could take up a whole book in and of itself, so I won't go into it too much here. When discussing cosplay, the question of its ritualistic elements is not something I want to be taken out of the specific context of cosplay itself. What I mean is that often people assume cosplayers are a strange social 'Other' who take fiction far too seriously and have the wrong levels of intention and ideas. I do not think cosplayers are psychologically questionable, nor do they pursue cosplay at the risk of rent and food – though some of the younger cosplayers I spoke to may have different hierarchies of financial importance. But I think this view of cosplay is reductive and not actually all that accurate. I acknowledge that relating cosplay to ritual may risk falling back into this mindset, but I hope to avoid that.

Cosplay as ritual does not necessarily mean (a) cosplayers are unable to have their own religious beliefs separate from cosplay, nor does it mean (b) cosplay is an inherently religious act. If we follow religious studies scholar Catherine Bell's view of ritual, it is simply marked as different because it distinguishes itself from other actions as something special. Bell also uses the term 'ritualisation', which refers to the process of something being seen or crafted as ritual.[13] Essentially, ritual does not have to be inherently tied to something that is recognizably a 'religion' in order for us to conceive of it as ritual.

We can see how this impacts our understanding, as more colloquially we use ritual in similar ways. I have many friends who talk about their 'rituals' associated with watching a particular show, or we all have heard the stories of football fans repeating rituals in the hope their favourite team will win. These instances do not have to do with attending church services, for example, but are actions we understand as something special, even if someone from the outside observing us doesn't see anything different or special. Perhaps a good example is a regular date night I have set up with my husband.

Typically, on Fridays, we have homemade pizzas and we indulge in our weekly dessert. I say weekly dessert, but we often cave in and buy sweets throughout the week, because we both have a sweet tooth. And yet, even if we have had desserts every other day of the week, the Friday dessert feels different because it's become a special day and moment in our relationship. We have a ritual for Friday, one shared between us as a family. Associating ritual with cosplay does not necessitate a connection to religion, but it does necessitate an understanding of something wonderful and special happening for the people partaking in the act.

Another important part of Bell's view is the function of ritual as helping to solidify our beliefs and understanding of the world through doing it. While this may seem like a bit of a stretch for cosplay, it actually isn't. Cosplay is an acting out of something inherently mythic – pop culture as myth helps to substantiate our ideas of what is important to us and those close to us. For many of the cosplayers I spoke to, the act of dressing as their characters helped them to feel closer to the narratives they love, to the characters who represent them or show them something important in their lives. By dressing as these characters (and performing, if they do this), they are actively solidifying feelings and beliefs that are reflected in the narratives they love. A good example is from one cosplayer I spoke to, who was cosplaying an autistic character. They told me how powerful and meaningful it was for them to see autism on screen in a positive and realistic way, especially because the cosplayer is autistic. Through this character, they were able to see a reflection of their own experiences and way of seeing the world.

Performance is an important part of this. But before we move on, I want to take a moment to talk about performance in relation to cosplay, ritual and mythic performance. One of the questions

I asked all my cosplayers was what cosplay was to them, and how it is different from other forms of 'dressing up'. Most talked about Halloween and the way some people will dress as fictional characters for Halloween, but many of these people drew a strong distinction between Halloween and cosplay.

John Emigh, who wrote about the role of play in masked rituals, has something interesting to add. Emigh noted there is a substantial difference between a masked performance that is ritual and a masked person who is simply just masked. For Emigh, a performance that mimics the appearance of the figure of the mask but does not replicate other aspects of the character, such as action and voice, is merely 'referential', and he directly refers to Halloween here.[14] I think this is an important element of cosplay as well. While the levels of performance may be different between cosplayers, there is always something more to cosplay than just donning a mask. There is some other kind of replication, some other kind of connection that draws the self into the cosplay – something which may be akin to ritualistic mythic performances.

Cosplay may, on the surface, appear as a light-hearted aspect of dressing up. I remember when I had a conversation with someone about this project while I was researching, we started chatting about the intricate and complicated nature of cosplay. The individual I was speaking to, near the end, said, in surprise, 'I guess it's more than just dressing up, then.' It is important to note that there is no such thing as 'just' dressing up. Dress itself has a detailed sociology that helps us demonstrate to others who we are, and it's all on our body, which is also read and understood on a variety of different levels such as gender, race, dis/ability and economic status.

The history of cosplay is long, and potentially much longer if we continue to look down the history of mythic performances. But even if we don't, it's far longer than just the 1980s and '90s, and mostly it is because people have always intuitively known the importance of dressing the body, and the way this communicates a variety of beliefs, ideas and actions.

We think of things as special; we have specialized actions and thoughts and beliefs and connections to our mythic fictions. And dressing as this fictionalized 'Other' can change us, because our body and our dress are an important way of communicating ourselves. Changing these things can actively change the way our identities are understood and read by others. There is something more about masked performances than just wearing a mask. Likewise, there is something more about cosplay than just wearing a costume.

3

Cosplay and the Art of Performance

S am was sitting in a small room, which they said was their child's bedroom. While sitting, they moved about on their chair excitedly as we talked about cosplay:

> When I did Harley Quinn, I embodied Harley Quinn and everyone loved it. They were taking recordings of me and trying to get me to break character and I just wouldn't break character no matter what someone said. It was pretty fun. Especially at the convention because that one I got to do multiple things. It wasn't just the costuming, it was the acting, the getting to be around other people, because there was someone who was Two-Face. So I was like [Sam switches to a mock high-pitched Harley Quinn voice, putting on a thick New York accent] 'Oh look Two-Face, you brought both halves: your good side and your bad.'

Like many cosplayers, Sam sees their art in the performance of the character first and foremost. In fact, some academic definitions of cosplay have described it as a type of 'performance art'[1] – ascribing performance as a primary mode of being. And there is much to defend this view of cosplay, especially when you chat to people like Sam.

It doesn't take long being around cosplay to start thinking about aspects of performance. If you're at a fan convention, ask a cosplayer for their photo. If they consent, they often immediately strike a pose, trying to replicate the type of stance you may see their character in. One cosplayer at MegaCon in Manchester, cosplaying as a character from the video game *Bloodbourne*, drew a giant mallet and held it as if ready to attack. Another, cosplaying as the child Anya from the Japanese anime *Spy × Family*, held her doll and looked demure and yet excited in the way only children seem to be able to – even though they were an adult.

Some take their performance beyond the poses for happy cameras. One of my participants, Mia, spoke with a bit of exhaustion about Deadpool cosplayers who take the opportunity to act over the top and are annoying. While Mia seemed to dislike this, it seems not to have stopped many cosplayers. While waiting for MegaCon Manchester to open, my partner and I were in the queue ahead of a Deadpool cosplayer who had decided to bring a small speaker with them, and blasted music and danced to the joint amusement and annoyance of those around them.

Despite Mia's irritation at Deadpool cosplayers, they also voiced how important it is to play the character accurately. 'Sometimes you see Sasuke cosplayers,' they said, referring to a character from the popular Japanese anime *Naruto*, 'and they're jumping around and being silly. Sasuke wouldn't do that.' Here, Mia emphasized how necessary it is for cosplayers to perform their characters accurately and proficiently (perhaps even to the annoyance of others).

Sam's love for the performative aspect of cosplay was clear. Throughout our conversation, they constantly shifted voice to show off how they would speak while in cosplay to mimic the character or described how they moved around the convention in a specific manner. Again, referring to their Harley Quinn cosplay, they discussed doing photoshoots with a big fried-egg sandwich, a running gag in the comic books with the character.

Another participant, Charlie, used the performance of character as their way to distinguish between cosplay and 'just dressing up'. 'When you cosplay . . . you're in that costume for that person.

Érica (@erica. cosplays) as Anya from *Spy × Family* at MegaCon Manchester 2022.

And to me, that then means that you take on a little bit of their persona, and you're acting the way that they would . . . And like dressing up, you might be wearing something a bit more elaborate. But you're still you whilst wearing it.' Charlie later compared acting to cosplaying: a cosplayer is like an actor going on stage in full costume. An actor has to perform as their character to be convincing for the show. A Halloween costume, however, would just be something you can throw on but you don't have to perform in.

Despite Charlie's comparison to actors, there are some differences between performing as a character in cosplay and performing as a character as an actor. In many ways, cosplay intentionally blurs the typical boundaries between the performer and the character being performed. Unlike an actor, the cosplayer's audience directly interacts with them as both actor and character simultaneously.

When interacting with cosplayers at cons, individuals chat to cosplayers as people wearing costumes half the time. Many cosplayers talked about their enjoyment of someone coming up and talking about the quality of their costume or asking for poses – ways of interacting that are not within the realms of acting as the character. But other cosplayers, like Sam, embody the character and interact with congoers as their character. For some cosplayers, they play both roles – flipping back and forth between their character and themselves fluidly.

At one con in Weston-super-Mare, a group of cosplayers dressed as Storm Troopers from *Star Wars* interacted with children who were cosplaying Jedis. They would call in about spotting a Jedi on their radios, and then play-acted being attacked by the children-Jedis. Another of their group, cosplaying as Darth Vader, suddenly appeared and pretended to force-choke one of the Jedis, who obediently acted as if being force-choked. After the child managed to escape their grasp and attack Darth Vader, they then all posed for a photo together.

The group of *Star Wars* characters was able to shift fluidly from cosplayer when walking around, to character when first interacting with the children, and then back to cosplayer at the end point of their play. Even my participants who were not as enthusiastically in character as Sam would discuss some level of shifting into character representation. Elliot, for example, spoke about how they never really acted as the character at all – they only cosplay for the enjoyment of wearing the costume. But even they mentioned flipping into character to pose for photos, or considering aspects of the character when making choices about costume construction.

Group of *Star Wars* cosplayers interacting with children in cosplay at
Stars of Time 2022, Weston-super-Mare.

Richard Schechner, a scholar in the academic study of performance, once made the distinction between make believe and make belief. For Schechner, 'make believe' is when the boundaries between what is real and what is pretend are maintained, while 'make belief' purposefully blurs these boundaries.[2] While some cosplayers, like Sam, would see cosplay as falling under 'make believe', where they have maintained the elements of character and are performing them as an actor would, other cosplayers are different. For them, cosplay falls under the category of 'make belief' – as cosplayers shift between pretend and not-pretend so smoothly, it purposefully blurs the boundaries. This is not to say, however, that cosplayers are unaware they are engaging with fiction – this is a simplistic and damaging idea about how people's understanding of the blurred boundaries is actualized. Rather, they are engaging in a type of play called 'as if' – in other words, cosplayers play 'as if' they are truly the character . . . sometimes. This performed belief is not a kind of dangerous level of understanding of reality, but rather a conscious decision made by cosplayers in order to extend the pleasure of cosplaying for both them and their audiences, as well as an ability to apply aspects of what they learned during this experience in cosplay to their non-cosplay life.

This can be compared to other forms of fun 'as if' play in popular culture, such as fans of wrestling and the rules around kayfabe – a term used to refer to the illusion of the narrative. Televised wrestling, such as World Wrestling Entertainment, is often entirely made up – the winners and losers are already decided, and certain wrestlers play types of characters who are either the heroes (faces) or the villains (heels). This is not to say there isn't an art to wrestling, or even an athletic requirement, but the storylines of wrestling are preset and not determined purely through the skill of the individuals. Most – if not all – fans of this type of wrestling are aware of the fabricated narratives but endeavour to maintain the facade, as that is what the type of storytelling calls for. Fans will condemn wrestlers and fans who 'break kayfabe'. So, if two wrestlers are supposed to be feuding in the story, but then one takes a photo of them hanging out together off-stage, the fans will claim this is breaking kayfabe, as the story would insist these two would not be having fun outside of the ring if they are feuding.

Again, fans of wrestling are aware of the boundaries between the narrative world and the reality of the wrestlers themselves. But the 'as if' play is important to maintain. Audiences are able to balance the different views and interpretations of the events as both play and reality simultaneously.

Cosplay performance does not necessarily need to be in mannerisms. For many of the people I talked to, the most important part of the performance is the costume itself. The choices made in the assembly of the costume are an important part of the performance and understanding of character. My participant Elliot, for example, talked about taking creative licence with the costume, but only within the confines of what is 'normal' for the character. This was echoed in many of my interviews – cosplayers stressed the need to perform the character 'accurately', even when making alterations to the costume, such as shifting the character's gender or making more sexualized versions of the costume. In most cases, 'accurate' was not in terms of body but rather in terms of character or personality. Being accurate to character was being true to the way the character would genuinely act. Everything else was more or less for the cosplayer to decide and put their own spin on.

In their performance, cosplayers embody aspects of the character and the story. In conversation with me, my participant Emma talked about how they sometimes are drawn to new stories they haven't engaged with before purely through seeing a cosplayer. Like Elliott, Mia stressed the importance of making sure the performance of your chosen character is accurate to the character itself, even when diverging from the character's appearance.

At the start of this book, we talked about how cosplay related to the conception of mythology – understanding cosplay as a performance of our contemporary mythology. The performative aspect of cosplay helps to demonstrate the connection cosplay has with myth and mythology. Myths are not just spoken or read. We often think of myths as old stories written in old books, but this isn't how mythology has historically been understood. Myths are also performed. Storytellers would act out tales in great halls or village street corners. Religious adherents would don masks to perform the great acts of well-known narratives.

Cosplayers, then, can be like the storytellers who donned masks, though instead of masks they use wigs and make-up (as well as masks sometimes), and the cultural narratives they tell are those which play on our cinema and television screens. Costume construction, wigs, attention to make-up or masks, and mannerisms and ways of speaking are all part of the cosplay performance, though each is given different levels of attention and care depending on the individual. No matter where the cosplayer focuses, accuracy to story is paramount. The cosplayer is telling a story, even if it's the brief element of characterization present when posing for a photograph.

This is not to say that cosplayers do not put their own spin on the characters. Cosplayers actively make choices to alter characters in small or big ways, depending on what they want to do. Some even change the character's gender, which we'll explore in Chapter Seven. Others change aspects of the character to fit the cosplayer's own experiences. For example, Black cosplayers often use wigs that mimic the texture and styling of Black hair to suit their own experiences, body and interpretation. Similarly, old storytellers of old myths would also make alterations to narratives in their own telling to fit their experiences, intentions or interpretations.[3]

Both cosplaying and mythic masked performances are processes of personification – the becoming of another. That 'Other' may be a figure in ancient stories, or it may be in popular culture. Either way, the process of dressing creates a connection between the performer/cosplayer and the character being embodied. The presence of the mask – or the costume for the cosplayer – is a moment of transgression, a shift in categories from one 'being' to another one, even if only temporarily and even if only in play. The mask demonstrates the marker of this transgression of categories.[4] It is through the mask that the individual is able to alter the way they are perceived by others.

Let's explain it another way with the example of a performer donning a mask to temporarily become a mythic figure for the purposes of storytelling or ritual. Before putting on the mask, the performer and the figure are two separate beings – two separate categories. We have the physical world – the actor – on the one hand, with the mythic world – the figure – on the other. The actor then puts on a mask and begins to act out the role of the mythic figure. During that time, the audience and the actor are both temporarily transported to a different state. The shifting of mythic time and physical time, also tied to the shifting of the figures, means that – at least during the time of performance – the two typically separate categories are blurred. This special performance revels in the world of these two typically very separate categories becoming one intimately tied together.

Something similar is happening with cosplay. We typically think of the fictional world and the physical world as being separate categories and locations – the two shall never be muddled. However, the donning of the mask and the performance of the character mean, for this one special moment, the separate categories of fiction and physical reality are connected, and we can play in the revelry of our favourite screen pastimes becoming physically manifest.

Myths, and stories more broadly, are a lot more than just the written word. Anthropologist of mythology Claude Lévi-Strauss alluded to two types of myth: the explicit myth, by which he meant the written myth, the words spoken or read; and the implicit myth, by which he meant the myth as it is performed or lived through life. In other words, Lévi-Strauss separated the words of the myth from the ritual associated with it.[5] But what was most telling in Lévi-Strauss's separation of the two is how he associated the separation with a hierarchy: the explicit – the words – being far more important than the implicit – the performance.

Others after Lévi-Strauss have adjusted this conception of the divide between the explicit and implicit, particularly to make it less hierarchical. Jacques Galinier, for example, described his time among the Otomi (an indigenous group in Mexico) and demonstrated how, for them, ritual – or the implicit – is considered of the same importance as, or maybe even greater than, the explicit written myth.[6] Jonathon Miles-Watson also adjusted the conception to be less hierarchical. He defined the implicit myth as that which both inspires and develops personal narratives of experience. In fact, for Miles-Watson, implicit mythology is more contextually situated, and therefore is capable of dealing with the problems involved in navigating the world.[7] What he means is that the physical world – including how we interact with it, especially in relation to the stories we tell – is more directly around us and therefore more easily able to answer the same questions faced in explicit or written mythology.

Cosplay, then, is the physically manifest implicit mythology. It's the performance of the story which we typically think of as only the written or spoken word. Bringing the myth to the physical world around us means we are able more easily to contextualize its presence in the world around us.

Let's use a different non-cosplay example and go back to the participant mentioned in Chapter One who had the tattoo of the Triforce from *The Legend of Zelda* series on their arm. While not cosplay, this is an act of implicit mythology – bringing the written script of the myth to life in the form of the ink on their forearm. The implicit mythology becomes contextualized into the everyday life of that person, who now uses the themes and conceptions from the written explicit myth in their life. It helps them to make decisions, to navigate the hard parts of life in a slightly easier way.

How this works for cosplay more specifically is equally complicated, and also dependent on the individuals. Just as not every fan of *The Legend of Zelda* games tattoos the Triforce on their arm, not every fan cosplays, nor does every cosplayer feel the same about the explicit myth they are drawing on. This means the way they understand their performance – the implicit myth of the piece of pop culture – is also slightly different for each person.

We see how this can work for some of our cosplayers. Sam, for example, told me about their interest in cosplaying a character from the anime *Fruits Basket* who was dealing with the grief of losing their mother. Sam, too, had lost their mother, and so wanted to cosplay as this character to better connect to someone who was dealing with grief in a way Sam wanted to replicate. Sam explains, 'When you resonate with a character, it usually makes it easier. Because I did find it harder at first that when I picked a character that was someone that I'm not that I wanted to be, it's kind of hard to pull yourself away from you and be them. So it's usually easier if you pick someone who's a little more with you.' Riley had a harder time putting their connection to character and how it forms into words, but expressed how important they feel their connection to character is: 'But if I – I psychoanalyse myself, even for a second, I'm like, I think these are just characters that I resonate with on some degree, emotionally.' Adrian, likewise, discussed how their best cosplays were ones where they had some emotional connection to the character.

Emma also feels connections to their characters. In fact, they expressed how they felt the most like themself when they were in cosplay. This was such an important facet of their life that it actually came up in therapy. 'My therapist actually knows about, like, cosplay and everything,' they said, and giggled at the admission:

> She said something that kind of struck me . . . She told me . . . 'I feel like you feel really comfortable cosplaying the character because you are that character. You literally feel like that character. So when you're cosplaying at cons and everything you're literally just being yourself . . . in the form of that character.' I feel like she kinda has a point.

Emma's performance in cosplay is much more complicated than a simple replication, but one that involves the understanding and performance of self. While the cosplay may be a mask, the mask becomes part of them. They have formed such a relationship with the mask that it's not just a representation of the fictional 'Other', but a reflection of themselves.

In this sense, cosplay performances are not just performances of fictional characters, but performances of the cosplayer as well. Mason talked about how cosplay is a transformation of the self, and how this can assist with easing emotions:

> You kind of transform into who they are. When you put that costume on, you become that person and other people see you as that person. And I think it's really nice to kind of live out that fantasy for a bit. So if you see someone ... really like a character in a really, like, nice environment and you're quite stressed, you're like, I can cosplay that character. And I'll feel cool and nice and chilled.

Photography is another important place in which cosplayers perform their characters, their costumes and their connection to narrative. At its most simplistic, this happens when other fans at conventions see their favourite characters and ask for a photo of the cosplayer. Cosplayers will typically suddenly adjust – dropping bags of personal belongings, adjusting any props to be within frame and striking a pose that's reminiscent of their character. When at a con, I noticed how different poses could be between characters. A cosplayer who was emulating anime character Violet Evergarden – a character struggling with depression and post-traumatic stress disorder – simply stared blank-eyed at the camera, body stiff and holding a bag. Their pose was very similar to the blank, empty of emotion look the character would often have in the show. In comparison, a cosplayer from the video game *Bloodbourne*, wearing a large black overcoat and wielding a giant hammer, posed as if getting ready to swing their weapon at the camera – which also happened to show off the fake blood splatters on their coat.

When I was cosplaying, I was not often asked for my photo to be taken. My costume went more or less unnoticed, or uncommented, by other con attendees. While cosplaying at MCM London 2023, though, I met another person cosplaying as a different figure from the same anime as my character. We both got excited to see a similar cosplayer because of how infrequently we saw these cosplays. When they asked for a photo with me, I was so excited that I smiled next to him. It wasn't until after the photo was taken that I realized the other person had struck a pose reminiscent of the character. Instead of posing like my character, I had been brightly smiling. I hope I didn't ruin the person's photo attempt at replicating the characters' personalities. This instance really shows how practised the person I was photographing with was at posing for photos, while I wasn't as used to it, as practised or as knowledgeable about telling a story with my body.

The cosplayer's initial inspiration point is from an existing piece of popular culture, and their poses and experiences in front of the camera always refer to the original piece or character. Even when cosplayers change the character in some way to fit their own conception, the poses help to point the viewer towards the original character. When posing as a female version of the urban fantasy book character Harry Dresden, a cosplayer still posed similarly to the front cover of the books despite the shift in gender, for example.

When I was researching and writing this book, I found myself inevitably in the position where people would ask what I was writing about now. If they didn't know what cosplay was, I would find myself clumsily trying to explain. About 90 per cent of the time, I was able to say 'like at Comic Con' and everyone suddenly understood. In fact, the presence of cosplay at cons is so connected that cosplayers are often stressed in the weeks leading up to attending a con. 'Con crunch' is the term cosplayers use to describe late nights – or completely sleepless days – spent trying to finish a costume in time to wear at a con.

However, as the Internet continues to grow and gives space to ever more community groups, cosplay has been living more and more online. During the COVID-19 pandemic lockdowns, people who once only cosplayed at cons suddenly found a place to practise their cosplays online when fan conventions weren't happening. Several of my participants talked about COVID-19 being the reason they shifted to having an online presence at all – they needed somewhere to cosplay.

Instagram and TikTok have become the two primary locations for cosplayers to find both a community and an audience. TikTok combines the performance typically seen at cons with the performance of simply being in costume, along with the trendy TikTok performances proliferating throughout the entirety of the platform. For Instagram, the art of the photograph reigns supreme. Photography has become so much part of the art of cosplay that many photographers will spend full days at cons simply taking photos. One photographer told me they had slots throughout the day people were booked into. As I tagged along with them, they rushed from area to area to meet with cosplayers and take their photos.

Like the cosplayers, most of the photographers, including the one who graciously let me follow them along to a large number of their shoots, were hobbyists. They had day jobs often completely unrelated to their love of photography. One, for example, worked for the police. Another told me they have few days off they can

Cosplayers @hadrianysia and @kurochuu_ getting their photo taken by
Nigel of Cosplay Academy.

take every year that aren't already reserved for cons. And the time photographers take for their hobby is not only the time at fan conventions. They spend weeks or months going through the photos and editing them to be of an incredibly high standard.

Because both sides of the photograph are hobbyists, most often they partake in what photographers call 'time for prints' – in other words, in exchange for the cosplayer's time as a model, the photographer would provide them with the prints. No money changes hands between the cosplayer and the photographer. A lot of the cosplayers I spoke to said they tended to avoid photographers who charged money for the prints unless they had very little choice otherwise. The photographers voiced annoyance at cosplayers who wanted to charge money to be a model, and seemed against charging money themselves despite the amount of time they had sunk into their own art.

Interestingly, this was a primary point of difference between cosplayers in the United Kingdom and the United States. While there were some photographers who charged in the UK, these were a minority. In comparison, in the USA there seemed to be more money changing hands. Cosplayers there talked openly with me about the amount of money they would spend on photography shoots and the difficulty in finding photographers they enjoyed. Sam, a cosplayer in the USA, expressed how they avoided photographers in order to keep their cosplays cheap. They explained that typically, for their area, it would cost about $30–40 for only a thirty-minute shoot where they received ten images at the end.

I think the difference is mostly due to the size of the two countries. The USA stretches across a much larger geographical area than the UK, and therefore the cosplay communities are more geographically restrictive. A small community of cosplayers and those adjacent to the community – like photographers – are far more spread out, and therefore impromptu meetings between cosplayers and photographers can be more difficult. In comparison, the UK community, while still relatively small, is also more tightly packed and it is easier to meet others regularly.

As the famous phrase 'a picture says a thousand words' indicates, photography is a form of storytelling. We can hear a full story in a photo. According to folklorist Jay Mechling, photography, particularly non-professional photography, can be understood as a type of folk performance.[8] Richard Chalfen discussed how photographs function as a form of visual communication and a mark of social activity.[9] He commented on how photography, particularly family photographs, are almost like statements rather than simply pictures. They communicate so much and can function as both a report of what was happening as well as an interpretative understanding.[10]

Cosplayers utilize the communication of photography to further their performance. A cosplay photograph must communicate not only the costume itself, but the stories which lie behind the costume, both the narrative of the original piece of popular culture and the narrative of the cosplayer's own interpretation of that character. A good example of the different forms of narrative which can come from one photograph is best exemplified in 'Olly Rose's cosplay of BB8 from *Star Wars* (see colour section, p. 129). Unlike other cosplays, 'Olly elected to choose a droid character, one who is normally understood as a simple whirling ball. They chose to bring the droid to a more anthropomorphic form, while still maintaining many aspects of the character's personality. The tilt of their head and the slight smile on their face allude to the playful energy of BB8. Along with their costume, which is taken directly from images of the droid in the films, their whole body communicates the story of BB8. But it also communicates the type of BB8 which may exist if they were anthropomorphized – and the viewer of the photograph buys into all of it from the single image. In this example, the cosplayer is definitely an important part of the storytelling process. As the model, the cosplayer must think about the whole performance of the body to communicate their story in the photograph. But the photographer is equally as important in the production of the image.

Photographers find many different routes to the cosplay community, but are not cosplayers and therefore exist somewhere on the boundaries of the community. They have an important role, but only during one part of the process rather than throughout. As more photographers become involved in the ever-growing cosplay scene, there is also a lot of concern for safety. Cosplayers frequently communicate 'red flags' involved in meeting photographers, and push for cosplayers to be safe when suddenly embarking on the role of model.

Photographers, too, ensure they push for safety for both themselves and the cosplayer when forging new relationships. One photographer I spoke to stressed that they never agree to shoot someone new outside of a con environment. Cons provide a neutral location. They never leave the main areas of the con with new cosplayers as well, allowing the cosplayer to feel comfortable surrounded by people. It takes several shoots with someone before the photographer would agree to meet outside of these constraints. 'It's as much for my own safety as theirs,' they told me.

The relationship between cosplayer and photographer is built up slowly and with a necessary condition of trust. Following a particular cosplayer for an afternoon, I observed one shoot where the cosplayer was familiar with the photographer. The shoot was inherently collaborative. The cosplayer showed images of their character that they liked, and the photographer explained small things which could help make the photo as similar to the inspiration piece as possible. There were two cosplayers involved in the shoot, a duo cosplaying as Cloud and Aerith from *Final Fantasy 7*. The Cloud cosplayer was shorter than Aerith, so the photographer staged Aerith in front of a rock Cloud was able to use to stand on to appear taller in the photo. Between shots, the two models shifted slightly between each picture, and also were able to interrupt to offer a different pose to the photographer. In contrast, the two also shot later with a photographer who was new to them. The posing seemed more stiff, and one of the cosplayers was clearly more uncomfortable with this photographer's direction than the earlier one.

The first photographer had gushed to me about the amount of times they had shot the two cosplayers and how they always liked shooting them. I asked if it was because of the quality of costumes or props (which was high), but the photographer stressed they didn't actually care about that. They were good models, and their relationship helped to create a comfortable environment for both of them. This was enough for the photographer to go back time and time again.

There is another aspect of performance which occurs sometimes at conventions: the cosplay competition and/or masquerade. In these performances, cosplayers parade on stage, either posing or acting out skits. Often, this is set to music, where performers either dance, move or pose on different parts of the stage. In others, they

Cosplayer screaming during their performance at the Cosplay Masquerade at MegaCon Manchester 2022.

play scenes from the show where the cosplayers lip-sync. In most competitions, cosplayers are judged on two factors: their skill in costume construction and their performance of character. Skill will be discussed more in Chapter Six, but the performance of characters on stage is also an important part of performance knowledge and action for a lot of cosplayers.

Performances on stage are often the best place for cosplayers to showcase their deep understanding of both the original material and the character they are cosplaying. Their choices of pose, music, sound effects or quotes are all made by the cosplayer for the sake of displaying their understanding. This can be done in two ways: displaying exact knowledge and displaying knowledge which can be altered. In the first case, cosplayers stick to original character without many alterations, while in the second, they tend to have fun with changing aspects of the performance for the sake of humour.

Not all the cosplayers I spoke to partook in competitions, but some did. In fact, for Mason, competitions were an important and a favourite part of cosplay: 'That's my main thing, personally. That's what I do. I'd love to make it my career,' they told me. 'You can do two minutes to get a song or a dance. I usually go dance . . . It's kind of like *Drag Race*, you can lip-sync and so yeah, they're really fun.'

Watching the cosplay performances on stage at conventions can be incredibly thrilling for audience members as well. Audience members interact with the performers by cheering, chanting and clapping to the beat. Often, cosplays from more recognizable media gets far more cheers than those that are not. But performers, regardless, always try to perform their character to the best of their ability.

Audiences are not only present for competitions or masquerades; they're also present for cosplaying more generally. In fact, when we think of performance outside of cosplay, there needs to be some kind of audience. Cosplay audiences could be in the chairs watching a competition, or they could be viewing photographs on social media. Perhaps they are just other con goers who are not in costume. Cosplay audiences are also cosplay consumers.

Sometimes, the audience becomes part of the performance. I mentioned previously a small performance piece between someone cosplaying Darth Vader and a young child dressed as a Jedi. In this instance, while the child was also a cosplayer, they were both a cosplayer and an audience member. But the Darth Vader cosplayer, and many others, also interacted with children and adults who were not in cosplay. A very young child, perhaps only around two years old, was quite scared of Darth Vader. On hearing the child's fears, and also hearing their parent – who was trying to assure the child that no one would hurt them – they started heading over to the child. The parent play-acted warding the cosplayer away with a fake fight and the cosplayer left them, allowing the child to hug their parent in relief and feel more secure and safe. The Darth Vader performance therefore acted both with and to the audience of the parent for the benefit of the child.

Daleks, robotic aliens from the *Doctor Who* franchise, are another common sight at fan conventions. Sometimes they are remote-controlled. At other times, they are costumes which encase a cosplayer. The latter use their robotic voices to harass and otherwise interact with attendees, playing out typical phrases associated with the creatures.

Sam excitedly talked about how readily they engage and interact with their audience at conventions. Their pride at never breaking character demonstrated how readily they played with others at the convention, and how the audience took great joy in interacting back. Many cosplayers voiced how interacting with people at conventions is their favourite part of cosplay, particularly with young children who are excited fans of the characters they're embodying. Mason, for example, described the constant request for pictures from kids, typically at anime conventions: 'everyone wants photos with you. And it's kind of a normal thing that would kind of freak people coming to a con for the first time out when you get seven *My Hero Academia* children tugging on you like, "Oh my god, can I have a picture? I'm like, I love you so much." And they've never met you before.'

While shadowing a photographer at MCM London in 2023, we slowly started making our way down to the car park with a family dressed as the primary characters from *Monsters, Inc.* It took roughly 45 minutes to move only about 3 metres (10 ft) down the hall, as they kept being stopped for photos. Despite this, every pose was patient and well thought out.

Audience interaction can also involve prop work. At MCM London in 2023, a cosplayer in costume as the primary character in *Sweet Tooth* handed me a flier that mimics the fliers from the show. Cosplayers handing out props happened frequently. Someone cosplaying Moist from *Discworld* handed out handwritten letters to people who commented on and complimented their cosplay. Handing out props to audience members helps to reassert the character's performance and the way the character comes alive around the audience of regular congoers.

But audience interactions are not always positive. One cosplayer told a story about going to an anime convention as a character from a video game, which they knew wasn't ideal but was the cosplay they had at the time. An attendee followed them around the con demanding to know why they hadn't dressed from anime and insulting them for their choice. Another cosplayer voiced frustration at an audience member who tried to tell them the sword props they had weren't accurate to the costume – the cosplayer decided that the next time they cosplayed as the character they would carry two giant stuffed fish as their swords instead.

One cosplayer I spoke to told me that their most negative interactions regarding costume construction actually come from non-cosplaying audience members rather than from other cosplayers. Often, this is because the audience is searching for a level of 'authenticity' in the cosplays they look at. They can critique small aspects of the costume which aren't considered as accurate to the original character as the audience member thinks they should be. But sometimes, as my cosplayer participant told me, they will change aspects of the original on purpose. Sometimes this is for comfort, and sometimes for financial reasons. Changes to original costumes are not abnormal in cosplay, and yet some audience members are obsessed about authentic exactness – sometimes to the detriment of the cosplayer.

Pamphlet handed to me by a *Sweet Tooth* cosplayer at MCM London 2023.

Cosplayer The Saddest Eg Tart at MCM London 2023.

This intense need for the 'authentic' cosplayer also has an effect on cosplayers with different bodies to the original character they choose to play. Cosplayers who are a larger size, a different race or even a different gender than the original tend to face criticism from the non-cosplaying audience. One cosplayer explained they were often told that they weren't allowed to cosplay a certain character due to their size and race. One Black cosplayer said they received messages on Instagram suggesting they play characters who were terrible stereotypes of Black people. Another said they heard people always describe their cosplays as the 'Black' version of the character, rather than simply someone cosplaying their character. 'I'm not the Black version,' they said, 'I'm cosplaying that character. I just happen to be Black.'

A Muslim cosplayer spoke of their problems with cosplaying Captain America. Audience members from the United States contacted them to condemn them for their treatment of the flag – to them, someone wearing a hijab shouldn't wear the flag, and definitely shouldn't be representing Captain America.

Disabled cosplayers are often treated differently by audience members as well. Frequently this is due to a desire for the audience member to see what they deem to be the 'authentic' character, including the body of the character as well. Cosplayers with walking aids, for example, are frequently asked to hide them in photographs, or not to use them when getting their photo taken. Some cosplayers talked about how non-cosplaying congoers would steal their walking aids thinking they were props; one in a wheelchair was pushed to a different area of the con without their consent.

Similarly, different gendered bodies are approached in different ways. Some cosplayers choose to play the character in the same gender as the original character, regardless of the cosplayer's gender. Feminine cosplayers dressed as masculine characters are far less harassed at conventions compared to masculine cosplayers dressed as feminine characters. At one convention, I met a group of three cosplayers wearing the costumes of the three main characters in the Netflix reboot *She-Ra*. The person I was with commented on how 'sad' it was that the cosplayer dressed as She-Ra was a transman. They confessed it was sad to see such a beautiful model transition. Likewise, they seemed visibly uncomfortable by the cosplayer wearing Catra's outfit – a tight-fitting feminine catsuit which was being worn on a more masculine body. As I was with photographers, I asked if they planned on shooting the group because I was a fan of the *She-Ra* show – they responded, perhaps only the She-Ra cosplayer.

Performance is often a defined aspect of cosplay, both from academics studying it and from cosplayers themselves. For many, the performance of the character is their favourite part of cosplay. They moved about in their chairs with excitement, acting out the scenes they loved, or they gushed about their experiences on cosplay stages. Some put on voices for me, while others talked about prepping by putting on playlists inspired by their characters.

My own experience around cosplay left me impressed with how cosplayers had a wonderful ability to strike poses which instantly evoked the characters they wanted to present, and I even felt guilty when I felt I took away from that with my own pose. Cosplayers' ability to perform was both in their personalities as cosplayers and a skill that they had honed and practised.

Performance is not just at cons, but in photographs and on social media. Performance was, for many participants, what set cosplay apart from other forms of dressing up, and what made it special. Grayson, for example, defined cosplay as dressing as a character you love and then playing them out. Micah said cosplay was a form of expression. Arthur directly talked about cosplay as a performance.

What people choose to cosplay is also incredibly dependent on the audience and audience interaction. In this way, where the cosplay is happening is of utmost importance. Typically, cosplay is associated with places like fan conventions. Performance needs to have a space for it to take place, a location for the performance to root itself, whether this be at a con or online.

Cosplayer at Stars of Time 2023, Weston-super-Mare.

4

Cosplaying in Place

So far, we've discussed cosplay online and in convention spaces mostly in terms of performance. The performance of characters can change depending on where the space is. People cosplaying at conventions flow in and out of character easily – striking poses when necessary but happily chatting about the construction of costume at other times. Those posing for photographs or cosplaying online may consider the performance to be more about modelling for the pictures and so pay more attention to how the costume reads two-dimensionally rather than three-dimensionally.

When considering their costume, people spend time thinking about the place in which cosplay will occur. The cosplayer may, for example, be more aware of the necessary comfort levels of wearing a costume at a con, including the bags necessary to carry personal items which may not be part of the original outfit. The type of con may also impact the cosplay choice. While it isn't necessary to wear costumes which fit the theme of the con, many do try. This means someone will be more likely to cater to an anime convention with a costume from an anime. So, like cosplayers, we should consider the role of place.

The question of place has impacted the history of cosplay and the cosplay community. It originally became known through attendance at fan conventions. As noted in the Introduction, 'cos-play' as a term was coined by game designer Nobuyoki Takahashi after he first encountered the phenomenon in the United States in the 1980s.[1] Before cosplay was named, there was a long history of dressing up which may or may not be related exactly to cosplay itself. Jules Verne in 1877, for example, hosted a masquerade where guests dressed as characters from his stories.[2] People have always enjoyed dressing up, especially for a special occasion like a mas-querade ball or a fan convention. It has always been important to take care and consider dress when it comes to being in a special place. Dressing up became a distinct feature of fan conventions over time, leading to the globalization of cosplay after Takahashi publicized it. Cosplay, therefore, has a long history of being present in specific places. Whether it was attending a costume party in the 1800s or a fan convention in the twentieth century, people who dressed as fictional characters did so because the location allowed for others to look at and accept the act, and ultimately appreciate the art and effort of the costume and costumer.

Despite the popularity of cosplay at conventions, and the con-nections drawn between cosplay and fan convention attendance, we should take a moment to talk about how fan conventions have not been – and continue not to be – a safe space for cosplayers. Bailey discussed with me how in the early 2000s and 2010s cosplayers typ-ically identified themselves through their online usernames – when it was a fair bit harder for the average person to discover whom that name belonged to. This meant individuals were able to conceal their offline identities for safety. Cosplay names are still used, but more as a convention held over from the past than as a source of safety, mostly because of the plethora of online content which bleeds between accounts, rather than because cosplay is somehow safer.

While cosplay is more generally accepted and understood now, cosplayers still have to take care while attending conventions. Some viewers feel the 'performance art' of cosplay means they are able to touch the costume without permission, for example, which can be incredibly problematic when it is attached to someone's body. One cosplayer commented how people always feel they can touch their hair, for example. Another told me a story of how they were wearing a mask which made it difficult to see, and someone came up behind them and touched their back and shoulder, shocking the cosplayer and making them concerned for their safety.

Some cosplayers come to conventions with what they call a 'handler' – a non-cosplaying friend or family member who is more freely able to see and move through the convention hall to keep the cosplayer safe, as well as to hold items for them when asked for a photo or when the cosplayer wishes to purchase items in the hall. The primary use of a handler, though, is to keep an eye on the cosplayer's level of exhaustion and step in when needed. This is particularly needed for larger costumes that leave the cosplayer less able to push back on photos or to navigate the con effectively. Larger builds have a habit of being stopped regularly for photos, and this can make it harder for the cosplayer to take a break or get food because it takes far longer to get around. While at MCM London convention, I was helping at the *Cosplay Journal* booth when a younger cosplayer in a full Pikachu costume came up to the table. They asked the table how to keep people from asking for photos because they were exhausted and needed food. This cosplayer lacked a handler, someone to stop and say, 'Actually, no, we can't right now. Sorry.'

Some cosplayers are hyperconscious of which costumes they take to cons compared to the ones they reserve for virtual interactions and spaces. Because many cons are primarily focused on vendors in the hall, some cosplayers take great care to ensure larger costumes are not blocking the pathways or access to the booths, although some vendors still complain about large bulky costumes. An example of a vendor hall at MegaCon Manchester can be seen in the photo here. While the hallways between booths were quite wide, this isn't always the case, which can make the flow of people more difficult when cosplayers are in larger and more complicated costumes. Not everyone factors this into account, but it's a growing concern which does affect costume choice.

Often, the type of con is decisive when it comes to costume choice. As noted above, a cosplayer attending a convention primarily based around Japanese anime is more likely to attend as a character from an anime rather than, say, a video game. However, this is not

Attendees at MegaCon Manchester 2022.

always the case and many cosplayers will see fandom conventions as a chance to dress from any media. At one anime convention in New York City, for example, a cosplayer went as a character from the video game *Elden Ring*. Some non-cosplaying attendees, however, see it as overstepping boundaries when cosplayers attend wearing costumes from other sources. One cosplayer who dressed from a video game series at an anime convention was harassed by an attendee who followed them around, criticizing them for not coming in costume from anime. This, of course, also demonstrates how conventions are not necessarily safe spaces for everyone.

While people can cosplay any character at conventions, it is important for them to be recognized. Most discuss the importance of simply being happy in their costume, but there is a considerable deflation of joy when they go through a con unrecognized. One person told a story of being very happy with a costume, and then regretting everything about it when no one recognized the cosplay. I understand this feeling. I cosplayed as Chise Hatori from the anime *Ancient Magus' Bride* twice at MCM over two different years. The only time I was recognized was when someone dressed as another character from the same show came up to me, and that was only after having been on stage. It made cosplay almost feel like it wasn't worth the effort.

That being said, perhaps I should have taken into account some of the aspects of the larger conventions in relation to the costume I chose. While the anime is not exactly obscure, it's also not one of the larger, more mainstream shows. My costume may have been better suited to a smaller convention that was only for anime fans, where I was more likely to run into individuals who knew the show.

Conventions tend to be the place where many of the interactions between cosplayers and photographers happen. While some of the photographers told me they occasionally met up with cosplayers outside of cons, this wasn't frequent and was only with cosplayers with whom they had already established a long-standing trusting relationship. At MegaCon Manchester, an entire section of the show floor, roughly a sixth of the main hall's floor space, was dedicated to photographers. Several had set up lighting rigs, backgrounds and tripods to be able to take photos quickly and easily while still within the hall. Cosplayers were lined up, waiting to get their photos taken with the photographers present. Some other photographers took cosplayers to the side of the con, and many more were just outside, still on the convention centre's property, taking photos.

One photographer who chatted to me in April had already booked up their whole time at a convention in October. Conventions

Cosplayers getting their photo taken, while others wait, at
MegaCon Manchester 2022.

are typically the safest place for both photographer and cosplayer to interact when first getting to know each other. The convention gives them a very public place to meet, and a solid area for photography to occur without having to leave the site. A lot of the more recognizable cosplay photographers get free passes to conventions like MegaCon and MCM because their presence sharing the photos of cosplayers online brings a lot of press and cosplayers. This is less often the case in the United States, where press passes are reserved for larger journalistic companies. Cons often create sets so cosplayers can take their own photos or photographers can use the sets. Even smaller cons have small sets set up to look like *Star Wars* or other backdrops from popular culture for any cosplayer to use as a photo backdrop. Bigger cons, like MCM and MegaCon, had several sets of a variety of backgrounds for cosplayers to use to pose by themselves, with other cosplayers or with attendees. In the image

Set piece modelled after *Star Wars* at Stars of Time 2022, Weston-super-Mare.

Cosplayers posing in front of a set at MCM London 2022.

here, a group of cosplayers are taking a photo with children who also came in costume at MCM London in 2022, posing in front of a screened backdrop.

Despite cosplay being a prominent feature of all cons, some conventions or other fan gatherings are far more about the presence of cosplay and cosplay photography than others. In the UK, the annual CosXpo is a two-day cosplay-focused event that takes place typically on the University of Reading campus. The university's setting has many woodland areas in the grounds and botanical gardens, as well as old buildings, which all provide wonderfully varied backdrops for photos without needing to resort to green screens and sets. Likewise, the more recent SecretCon is another convention which is focused on the experience of cosplaying and photographing cosplays.

One person expressed to me the differing levels of stress they felt for the different types of conventions. For big comic cons, they felt they had to have not necessarily the best costume but rather the most recognizable. For CosXpo, they felt they had to have the most well made. CosXpo's focus on cosplay meant that many cosplayers were able to express affinity for costumes even when they didn't know the original character, which happens less often for cosplayers at larger fan conventions like MCM.

Blake confided how they believed CosXpo as well as other cosplay-centric events were responsible for boosting cosplay in the UK. 'The UK cosplay scene used to be kind of a joke compared to other places,' they said, referring to the fact that, compared to other areas of Europe, it was thought to produce lower-quality cosplays. They believed the gathering together of cosplayers purely for its own sake, rather than as an aspect of fandom more generally, allowed for it to flourish.

Conventions form a large part of the life and experiences of a cosplayer, as well as for the larger fandoms cosplayers are a part of. While conventions are not necessary for cosplayers to do their thing, it remains for many the only time they cosplay. Conventions are also for many the best part of cosplaying because of how social the events are for the individual and the community.

Bailey explained to me that it was at a convention that they first discovered cosplaying as something they could do. Bailey described seeing a group of women dressed as *Warhammer* characters. 'I'm not entirely sure if they were LARPers or cosplayers, or whether they were a bit of both.' Bailey was quite young at the time, and the older girls were nice and chatted with the young attendee, having fun conversations about their collective interests and answering questions about their costumes. 'They, like, talked to me for ages, for my dad and my brother went off to do something that I wasn't interested in. And yeah, they just talked to me for ages. And they were really nice and welcoming.'

Bailey also described the first time they were able to go to a convention without their parents, promising to attend with several friends:

The people I went with all abandoned me. One of them was not meant to be going out with a certain boy. When we met, [they] went, 'Oh, yeah, this entire thing was an elaborate ruse, so I could go meet my boyfriend.' I'm like, 'Okay, well, thanks.' And one of my friends could only stay for the first day.

By the second day of the con, Bailey was alone and so started hanging around new people they had recognized from the previous day. 'And then, weirdly, like the people . . . are still my best friends to this day.'

Cosplay scholar Nicolle Lamerichs described conventions using the idea of 'places of imagination'. This draws on the work of Stijn Reijnders, who in turn drew on French historian Pierre Nora. Nora coined the term *lieux de memoire* or 'places of memory'. The idea is that many historical locations around us become centres for collective memory, even for a memory we may not individually have. A social group begins to search into its past to find something which roots them all together. Their shared history is something in the past, and not something they can touch and feel and collect around in any physical sense. Because of this, monuments, museums and other centres of our past become places for this collective memory to thrive. These places become the physical presence which represents the less physical aspect of our social gatherings. This draws on an idea that humans need physical things which represent our non-physical ideas, thoughts and emotions.

Reijnders takes this as a jumping off point and pushes the idea of *lieux de memoire* a little further. Instead of focusing on memories, Reijnders examines *lieux d'imagination* or 'places of imagination'. He started with pop culture tourism – people who travel to different places that are depicted in fictional stories. Reijnders specifically looked at people who are fans of television detective stories, such as those who travel to see 221B Baker Street in London, the famous house of Sherlock Holmes, but I think many people would fall into this category.[3] People travel to Japan as part of a Ghibli experience, for example, or to New Zealand because of *The Lord of the Rings*. In the UK, there's a heavy presence of people traversing the English landscape to visit the many sites, both in the books and in the movies, linked to Harry Potter.

Reijnders notes that people need physical spaces to exemplify their collective memories or identities as a nation (or another kind of social group); others also need physical spaces to exemplify their shared imagination. People who travel to Platform 9¾ in King's Cross Station, for example, are under no illusion that Harry Potter exists. They know he is fictional, but it becomes as important as a monument for a significant historical event. The space becomes a physical tangible space for the non-physical collective imagination of those who love the fictional world it represents.

And here Nicolle Lamerichs picks up the idea. Lamerichs points out how Reijnders emphasized that individuals actualize stories through their shared imagination with others in the same fandom by visiting sites that are mentioned in, or directly related to, fictional narratives. For her, something similar happens at fan conventions. Rather than the convention's location being a place directly mentioned in fiction, it's rather a temporary meeting space for the fan group to actualize their collective imagination. In many senses, the location itself is not nearly as important as the ability to come together – the empty space of a convention hall is transformed into a space in which fans see their fictions come to life and walk the halls alongside them.[4]

Conventions differ from physical spaces like 221B Baker Street because the convention space itself is not really considered all that important. The physical location of the space isn't as significant as the physical construction of the space. In other words, whether MCM happens at the ExCel centre in London or in Birmingham isn't as important as the fact that it happens at all. The convention creates the physical space for individuals to make their connections. It's the space where the individual becomes communal. It's far more temporal than Platform 9¾, but the feelings of the community are intensified during the event due to its temporary nature.

The way individuals feel about conventions generally reflects what Lamerichs says about the actualization of imagination, fiction and community. I attended a fan convention in 2017 called CoxCon for YouTuber Jesse Cox. Despite the fact that I initially went in order to learn more about how fans engaged with his content on horror video games, I ended up only hearing conversation about the con itself. Attendees wanted to discuss everything about the event and share the excitement about just *being* there. I found many similarities between what they were saying and what both academics and pilgrims say about pilgrimage.[5]

The convention is the physical representation of the community, the moment the often virtual communities of fandom become physically present in the world around the attendee. This feeling of togetherness is constantly sought out by participants and reaffirms the presence of the community for them. At CoxCon, a participant told me they felt comfortable talking to strangers at the con because being in the same fandom meant they also had the same values. For those outside of fandom circles, this may seem a large leap to make of strangers, but the knowledge that the con is a reflection of the community more broadly helps to make sense of the feeling of togetherness. As Emma, one of my interviewees, expressed: 'That's the life of a con. You can be weird with other people and they're not going to judge you for it.'

Riley voiced a similar sentiment. Cosplay, for Riley, was often created in isolation, but the moment it comes into contact with the community something amazing happens: 'And then you take it to a space where actually loads of other people are doing the same thing. And all of a sudden, it's like, are these people like me? I have friends here. I have allies here. I have people who think and want to create in the same way that I do.'

Blake once told me that going to conventions around the world wasn't as strange as they thought it would be. They had expected to find a lot of differences, but actually cosplayers had a similar sense of language, values and community which made it easier to find comfort even in an unfamiliar space. 'Obviously there's going to be some cultural differences,' they said, but cosplay was a uniting factor that made them feel connected.

This is because cosplay is somewhat akin to Benedict Anderson's concept of the 'imagined community'.[6] This is not to say that cosplay's sense of community is not real or is made up by cosplayers, but rather that the connections between the community members are nonphysical and understood as inherently present between individuals and their sense of selves. It's the idea that a British cosplayer can meet a cosplayer in Japan and find a lot of similarities immediately because they are both cosplayers. We'll talk more about community and imagined community in the following chapter.

What the fan convention gives is an experience of many things cosplayers feel even when separated by space prior to and after the event: the similarity and connection to community, the relationships inherently present between individuals, and a physical manifestation of the collective imagination. This results in an intense actualization of community in the few days of the event space, resulting in a large explosion of emotion between the individuals.

The notion of cosplay as something which happens regularly and consistently at conventions creates added difficulties for those with less mobile bodies or who are disabled. Conventions are infamous for not being very accessible. They are loud and tiring even for able-bodied participants, making them often far too difficult for those who are not. The aisles of vendors can sometimes be narrow, making it difficult to move around or allow space for wheelchairs. The sheer numbers of people can also create environments which are difficult to move around in. Overleaf, we can see just how closely packed conventions can be. CosXpo 2022 had workshops and panels for cosplay information, but they were spread across multiple stories which often did not give enough time to get to the next panel even if you ran. It meant wheelchair users struggled to keep up, and often simply stayed in one or two rooms. I saw more wheelchair users at a different convention. When panels didn't have microphones, it meant some people were unable to

Crowded hall at MCM London 2022.

hear throughout the whole panel, and none of the conventions I attended had sign language interpreters for those who were hard of hearing or deaf.

Costumes can create added difficulty in moving at events which are already not very accessible. Able-bodied cosplayers sometimes choose the disabled bathrooms to change or alter costumes, making it difficult for disabled participants who need to use the stall. Others have to think about their ability to move and their mobility aids when deciding on their costumes to ensure they are able to get around the con.

Many disabled cosplayers told me they struggle with con organizers infantilizing them. One mentioned a family member who was able to get into the con for free by saying they were a caregiver, despite the cosplayer telling organizers they did not want that person there. Sometimes, disabled people cannot enter the con at all, even after purchasing a ticket, if the entry is upstairs with no wheelchair access.

Some aspects of cosplay itself can also be detrimental for both disabled cosplayers and disabled people more generally. Some able-bodied cosplayers will purchase second-hand mobility aids for costumes of characters who use these aids. However, these are *real* mobility aids, not props. Adrian, a disabled cosplayer I spoke to, complained to me about this:

> I have to, like, explain to people that those things new cost a lot of money. Most of the time, like, most chairs that the same people use are in the £500 and above [range]. If you want electric, it is in the £1,000 and above [range]. So a lot of people having health issues, whether they're permanent or not, rely on second-hand markets to get to the thing they need to be able to, like, go to work.

Adrian reflected that they were able to get their wheelchair for only £50 thanks to the second-hand market, and mentioned that they don't know if they would have been able to afford it new. Purchasing second-hand aids for the sake of 'props' means someone who needs that aid to actually move around is less likely to get what they need.

Disabled cosplayers also tend to be neglected at cons by the audience and other attendees as much as they are neglected by organizers. Adrian showed me a group photo taken at a con where there was a large gap between them and the rest of the group. Another disabled cosplayer discussed having their aids taken away from them by other congoers because they thought they were props, leaving the cosplayer stranded and unable to move. One cosplayer who uses a walking stick was asked for a photo, and then told to pose without their aid. When they said they would be unable to stand, the person taking the photo insisted on it anyway because the character didn't use an aid and they wanted the photo to represent the 'authentic' character. The use of aids can be very difficult for some cosplayers to think about. Stevie admitted to me that they put off using an aid for a long time due to the inherent ableism in both wider culture and in cosplay more specifically.

While at conventions, I frequently took photos both for myself and for others. At one event, for example, I was helping out the *Cosplay Journal* by taking photos of cosplayers around the convention on a Polaroid camera. I found while photographing cosplayers who needed mobility aids that they would hide the aid in photos. Despite insisting they didn't need to do that – especially one cosplayer who started to stand from their chair – many did because of what was often considered to be the expectation of the photographers.

Conventions can also be places of other forms of abuse and negative interactions for cosplayers. Many bemoaned to me how some people equate cosplay with a sexual fantasy, and sometimes make propositions or touch cosplayers inappropriately. Another told me that some who pose with him in photos will ask for consent to touch, but will often do so while already touching. Many cons have acted against this; several I attended had notices of 'Cosplay is Not Consent' in many locations throughout the con, for example.

Black cosplayers often encounter racism, both subtle and not very subtle, while at cons. One cosplayer told me about how they often heard people designate them as the 'Black' version of the character, such as 'the Black Goku', while white cosplayers are only ever thought of as their characters and not the 'white' version of them. Another Black cosplayer expressed how they often experience other attendees suggesting they cosplay only Black characters and rarely ever a white one, including several characters who are incredibly negative stereotypes of the Black body and culture.

Emma, luckily, had never experienced any racist remarks at the time they spoke to me, but they experienced the lack of interest in their cosplays in a different way. They expressed how when they started attending cons, they would find themselves as one of the only people of colour in attendance. But even now that there are slightly larger numbers, they find that people simply ignore them.

Some Black cosplayers openly discussed issues with arranging to meet photographers. While some do ignore them, others may set up meetings to photograph them and then pull out at the last minute. One mentioned that they felt it was because they showed up as a character from *Sailor Moon* and not a character who matched their skin tone. In fact, photographers, both the hobbyists and professionals, will often neglect Black cosplayers openly. One cosplayer told me about being in a group of cosplayers when someone asked for the group's photo, excluding them.

While cosplay has become a feature at fan conventions like MCM in the UK and Comic Con in the USA, these are not the only places in which cosplay is readily shared and experienced. Some people do not see themselves as being restricted by events when it comes to cosplaying. Elliot explained to me how they sometimes cosplay with their friends by simply walking around their town – not for an event or photography session, but just for fun. Adrian was the same, saying they enjoyed putting on their costume to go to a coffee shop or around town. Cosplayers are also able to connect and share their cosplays online. The Internet has provided another location in which cosplay is readily explored.

The cosplay community is spread out around many different areas online. More image-focused online spaces, such as Instagram, have a growing cosplay scene which allows users to connect to others in different parts of the world as well as providing an avenue through which to share their cosplays more generally. After editing the photos taken at cons, photographers will typically share their images on social media, tagging the cosplayers in the photo in order to distribute the image effectively.

More video-focused websites, such as TikTok and YouTube, offer other ways of sharing cosplays. YouTube fosters learning elements, such as 'how to' and other instructional videos for cosplayers to connect and grow their skill in the art of cosplay. Some YouTube videos on cosplay will also demonstrate the costumes in video form rather than in still images to show the movement and the life of the costume. This ensures that cosplayers think about the costume more three-dimensionally, as they would for a convention, rather than simply for still images.

TikTok has a variety of ways in which cosplayers connect, some of which is instructional like YouTube, but some of which is made to explore the more fun side. Cosplayers will put together small skits between different characters, or film themselves lip-syncing a song which fits their character or is sourced directly from the original material. Others follow specific TikTok trends both inside and outside the cosplay community.

The proliferation of social media, and other realms of the online environment, means cosplayers are able to become 'professional' cosplayers. I use professional in quotes for two reasons:

the first is that many professional cosplayers do not only cosplay, and the second because there is sometimes little difference in skill between professional and amateur cosplayers. Regardless, the growth of professional cosplay means there are even more cosplayers struggling to use the Internet in similar ways to create their own audiences and professional development.

The interconnected threads of the Internet also mean those who are creating professional pathways have their own ways of connecting multiple strands of income together. Jessica Nigri, for example, not only shares her cosplays online, but has an Only Fans account which helps to supplement her cosplay income, as well as other modelling gigs. Her online presence is able to connect all of these together in order to allow her audience to seamlessly flow from one strand of income to another without losing track of whose content they are consuming. Other cosplayers, such as Kamui Cosplay, for example, not only have modelling contracts but sell and make costumes for companies.

The rise of social media influencers who are cosplayers means some cosplayers feel pressure to be online. One cosplayer explained how they feel quite a lot of stress to stay up to date on Internet trends and create costumes quickly to match what's popular online and being searched for. They were starting to fade from that, though, as they talked about how hard it was to keep up and how they often lost sleep over trying. Most of the cosplayers I spoke to were not interested in being considered professional cosplayers, but a select few clung to it. One had only just recently given up on the dream and told me how liberating it was to suddenly be out of all the stress. Another, though, was still hoping to make it, and talked me through the time they spent searching online for popular search terms and keeping track of online trends, as well as attending as many conventions as they could to enter costume competitions.

The intense stress of social media also results in more eyes on cosplay, and therefore more comments from people – both positive and negative. One cosplayer told me they never wanted to get involved and get sucked into that life, so avoided social media entirely. Others simply make sure they don't fall into the pitfalls of social media stress. Riley, for example, told me they carefully curate their social media in order to restrict the number of followers. 'I just – I won't let myself get too many followers, too many – too much accolades,' they explained. 'I've seen it in other people, and friends of mine whose cosplays have like, reached like, quite a high viewing platform online. And then all of a sudden, you know, they get the horrible comments.' Emma equally expressed a lack of interest in becoming professional. They simply use their social media account to connect to the cosplay community when not at conventions.

Place and space are important considerations for cosplayers, from costume choice and construction to the way they feel about the growth and development of their own cosplays. But it also creates the environment for cosplayers to dive into the community of cosplay and fandom, and live in the ephemeral yet intense emotions of being part of the community.

Cosplay is most often associated with fan conventions like Comic Cons. Conventions themselves are the manifestation of a nerd culture community, and are the location in which the cosplay community can gather and engage with others who share their interest. Conventions become the manifestation of the community, and a place for the shared collective imagination to come to life.

There is a direct relationship between place and cosplay, which cosplayers always have to be consciously aware of. Whether the cosplay is online, at a convention or just around town, costumes are worn for the purpose of being seen in a place, and the location impacts the decision on what to wear – even in cosplay.

Despite conventions being such an important place for the community, they are not always safe spaces, especially for those from marginalized groups. Care is often taken on the part of both cosplayers and their friends and family to ensure cosplayers remain safe, fed and looked after during conventions.

While the cosplay community is a source of great joy for some, such as Riley, connecting them to a community of creativity, it can also be problematic in much the same way as the convention space. Because the convention space is a physical manifestation of this community, it makes sense that the nuanced and complicated nature of the convention space would also be a reflection of the nuanced and complicated nature of the cosplay community.

5

Cosplay's Community

Until now we have been taking the idea of the cosplay community for granted. People are cosplaying and talking to one another – therefore a community must exist. But that's not always the case, and things are not always that simple. So let's take a step back and think about what it means when we talk about the cosplay community. Is it cohesive? What are the boundaries? What are some of the experiences people have within this community, both good and bad?

The first step to figuring out who – and what – the cosplay community is to consider aspects of cosplay itself. Now that we've explored many dimensions of cosplay, we can pull back to examine, once again, what it means exactly to 'cosplay'; this will help us to question the boundaries of the community and consider in what realms the community belongs.

As previously noted, the term 'cosplay' is a portmanteau of 'costume' and 'play'. So in a more direct line from the term itself, cosplay would be any play with costumes. But this would include many aspects of the phenomenon of what I like to term 'dress play' – avenues through which individuals play with identities and performances using shifts in their attire. Other forms of dress play include acts like drag (where individuals dress as a different gender); live action role-playing or LARPing (where individuals dress as original characters in a world and act out their gameplay live in the world and in costume); historical re-enactment (where individuals dress and play with historical timelines and costumes); and nerdlesque (where individuals dress in costumes of fictional characters and then perform a burlesque routine), just to name a few. Each of these has its own relationship to costume, play and identity, and also a different relationship to cosplay, either in similarity or difference, or in the ways individuals may do both.

Probably one of my favourite questions to participants was for them to explain cosplay to me. I typically waited until we had chatted about a few different dimensions of cosplay before I proposed it. The role of an anthropologist is to be annoying, to pester with questions which seem simple and normal, but –simply through asking – point out what may not be so simple or so normal. We take things for granted, assume elements about both ourselves and others; the role of the anthropologist is to pick all this apart and consider what is happening with others and why it happens that way. When we are 'insiders' to a group, we think of some of the elements and boundaries and definitions as givens. As someone who grew up loving and enjoying 'nerd culture', I also took the idea of cosplay for granted. The differences between cosplay and historical re-enactment, for example, seemed obvious to me. But that was my 'insider' voice talking, and the anthropologist voice was less sure.

As I explained in the Introduction, in anthropology there are two different voices or perspectives we can talk about: the 'emic' voice or perspective and the 'etic'. The emic is that which is from the group we are studying – the 'insider' voice, for lack of a better term. The etic, on the other hand, is the scholarly way of thinking about it, the analytical side or the 'outsider' voice. In some circles,

COSPLAY AND THE DRESSING OF IDENTITY

one of these is typically privileged over the other, but I think you need a healthy dose of both to have a full and complete picture of what a community or group of people are truly like.

When I first approached the study of cosplay, for example, I was being influenced by my emic voice. While I hadn't cosplayed myself yet, I had seen it many times. I had taken photos of cosplayers at cons and looked at them admiringly on Instagram. I knew what it was and enjoyed it as an audience member. This perspective is important, because sometimes there are aspects of life that are just hard to put into clear rules and boxes. Not everything is always easily labelled and explained, but we feel it in our souls. In 1964 United States Chief Justice Potter Stewart said of pornography that although he can't define it, he knows it when he sees it. I think this is true of much of life: we struggle to define what we're looking at, but our deep cultural or social knowledge of what our communities expect of the world allows us to recognize it when we see it. This, of course, can lead to arguments when different worldviews start to realize they recognize different things at different moments.

From the emic perspective, I know cosplay when I see it. I also know historical re-enactment when I see it. But as an anthropologist, do I really see a difference? And what are the differences? However, too much of the analytical viewpoint from the outside observer without the knowledge and views of the individuals themselves reeks of the scholar who only sees the world from their viewpoint and does not listen to the people they are studying. We need to listen to others, but with a healthy dose of questions – not to prove people wrong, but so we can get at the heart of the way they see the world and categorize the elements within it.

Essentially, we anthropologists need to allow ourselves to be confused by the world around us. To be confused means we start to sort things out, and when we do that we can learn a lot about the way we understand the world. We understand who's in one group and who's pushed outside of it. Getting confused means things get weird, and getting weird means we learn and find the fun, creative and nuanced parts of life.

When it comes to 'costume play', we have a lot of options in front of us. We've got people dressing up as Spider Man for Comic Con in San Diego, but we also have people dressing in the costume of historic Saxons in the north of England, or a burlesque performer dressing as Princess Leia to do her routine, or even a child dressed as a pirate for Halloween. All of these involve aspects of playing with performance and identity due to the donning of a costume, but the reasons behind it and the performance will be different. So to be 'cosplay', one needs something a bit more than 'costume' and 'play'.

Let's take a moment, for example, to talk about drag. Drag is quite similar to cosplay in some respects. Like cosplay, it is a form of identity play while in costume – it is 'costume play' to an extent. But there are some primary differences between the two. Even when individuals cosplay characters who are a different gender – and the cosplayer does not alter this gender in their performance – then it could in some instances be construed as drag. In other words, if a female-identifying cosplayer dons a male-identifying character's costume and the cosplayer continues to perform the character as male, then in many ways a female performer is also performing a masculine identity – a gender performance comparable to drag. This particular instance was actually quite common among many of the female-identifying cosplayers I talked to. The reasons for their choice varied from individual to individual, including a desire to remain faithful to the original character and simply a desire for comfort.

The difference and similarity between cosplay and drag was a conversation point for many of the people I chatted to. Mason, for example, painted the primary difference as the way one engages with the material being worn. 'I'd say drag is an art expression,' they explained.

> I love drag, and it's like you're wearing a painting, or . . . I see it as there's different types of when you're doing drag: you could be doing a drag impersonation . . . or you're kind of your own OC [original character]. But with cosplay, I think you're – I think it's different because you're fully embodying a character that is already in the media. I guess drag, they kind of take the elements and get a plot twist on it. With cosplay, it's like you fully deal with the whole media.

What Mason is pointing out is how cosplay relies on a relationship and connection between cosplayer and the character's media. Arthur had a simpler view: 'Cosplay to me is a performance. For me, it is drag, but instead of portraying your own character, you're portraying someone else's character.'

For many cosplayers, the character performance and the performer are two separate entities. For the female cosplayers I spoke to who frequently play male-gendered characters, they still wish for their own identities as the cosplayer to shine through alongside the individual they are cosplaying. Referring to the cosplayer using the character's pronouns, for example, can be problematic. The cosplayer is not the character. This recalls aspects we considered in Chapter Three. There, we talked about how cosplayers negotiate their identity alongside their character. It is not that they perform

their characters wholly and completely – the vast majority of cosplayers shift between their character performance and their own
selves fluidly, dependent on each individual circumstance.

Historical re-enactment also provides a different form of
dress play. Individuals dress as historical figures – sometimes real,
sometimes fictional – and often also take aspects of the historical
construction of clothing into their own costuming. At first, the
boundaries between cosplay and historical re-enactment seem
firmly set: one is based on the history of our world, while the other
is based on fictional accounts. But I think this fails to consider some
of the more interesting aspects of cosplay.

While walking through a con for an online production company, I found many individuals cosplaying on-screen personalities.
This means individuals were cosplaying real people they were
going to see and potentially even talk to at the con. Cosplaying real
figures is not unusual. One cosplayer I spoke to talked about how
they had started by cosplaying famous DJs, such as Marshmallow.
While not historical, these instances of cosplay show that cosplay is not limited to fictional characters. Some cosplayers choose
types of characters, such as plague doctors, or dress as centurions.
Likewise, many historical re-enactors choose to create their own
characters who would have lived in the time and place they are
re-enacting. Despite being set in a factual location, the individuals are fictional. This thought experiment involves truly working
out the identity of the individual they are creating the costume for
and constructing a personal history involving family, all of which
is reflected in their clothes and the way they carry their body.

Nerdlesque is also quite a different take on dress play. As
stated above, it is a form of burlesque performance where individuals initially are dressed in the costume of a character from

Cosplayers Crafty Cosplay UK as centurions at MCM London 2023.

popular culture before removing the costume over the course of the performance. There is a lot of overlap between nerdlesque and cosplay – most of the nerdlesque performers I spoke to were also cosplayers, but this meant they distinguish between the two types of performance. Ms Pixy, a nerdlesque performer based in Chicago, described it as being a more traditional performance than cosplay. Nerdlesque was reserved for stages; the pairing with the burlesque routine meant it remained particularly distinct from cosplay. But the point of nerdlesque is to tell the story of the character chosen, or to describe a perspective on the character or story, all through the movement of the body and the removal of the costume. The character's story should not involve just the costume, but must be present in the body and the performance the body is undertaking.

LARPing, or live action role-play, is perhaps the most difficult to distinguish. I remember first being introduced to LARPing
through my experiences at university. When walking home from
the library, I was suddenly surrounded by a group of Jedi. While
I was accidentally in the same bubble, they were ambushed by a
group of Sith. Once others realized I was caught, they play-acted
getting a 'civilian' out of the fray. Because LARPing involves group
play in the physical world while pretending to be in a fiction, costumes are definitely a large component. Again, there was a lot
of crossover: several cosplayers also discussed their experiences
in LARPing communities, though most explained LARPing as
something they did when they were younger (if they were in their
late twenties or older), while those who were still at university
discussed occasionally partaking in LARPing.

We see the line between these various forms of dress play being
crossed in all sorts of ways. It can't just be fictional characters, nor
can it be based purely on location – as discussed in the previous
chapter. It can't be based on firm ideas of exact replication, due to
the frequent presence of alterations to the costume for a variety
of reasons for cosplayers, which we'll discuss in later chapters.
So how can we draw the lines between other dress plays and cosplay? Well, one way is by looking at how others have drawn these
boundaries. We can consider how other academics have looked at
cosplay, especially those who are coming at it from perspectives
other than anthropology to see if their views provide some new
understandings for us. This means we are looking at definitions and
boundaries drawn by the etic voice – the scholars who attempt to
stand outside and assess from this separate location.

But I, instead, choose to focus on the emic voice – the voice
of the individuals. This is not exactly new in research, but it is

important to stress here as it may prove to be very useful in defining the cosplay community. We should let go of the etic's outside perspective and instead focus on the emic, on what the people just living their lives, dressing up in costume, have to say about themselves.

What this means is we allow others to define themselves and where they see their own field's boundaries, and we abide by that. One of the interesting things that happens when we do this is we allow others to show us what they think cosplay is, and in that we also see debates between people. Maybe some think sexy cosplay isn't 'real cosplay'. Or maybe the way one does cosplay – like making your own costumes – is most important, which may rub those who purchase their costumes up the wrong way. If we draw our own boundaries first, we may miss some of these debates within the community, or cut out entire aspects of the community from our understanding and purview.

So how do we define the cosplay community? Well, I don't have a firm answer to that. But I do have something to say: the cosplay community is what cosplayers say it is, and functions the way the cosplay community describes. That's not to say the cosplay community is in any way cohesive, especially when discussing it across regional or national boundaries. Sam, for example, told me about their cosplay community and its impact on their family and life – but was primarily focused on the cosplayers in their area. Cosplay communities can be globally present online, but the close-knit connections drawn by Sam come from more regional relationships.

Sam described an important time their specific cosplay community gathered together. They have a son who had no one show up at their birthday party one year and was heartbroken. Sam said the son directly asked them, 'Why do people hate me?' The next year, Sam was determined not to let their son be left alone again and so told the cosplay community about the party, which was *My Hero Academia* themed. Sam made their son pyjamas to look like the main character. 'Well, I thought only like a handful of people were gonna show up,' Sam told me, 'but hundreds – we had like 200 people show up for this . . . for this little birthday.' Each attendant was in cosplay from the show and was happy to celebrate an eighth birthday with a child. 'It's just beautiful,' Sam continued. 'It really is – to know that we're not just like supporting each other, but also the next generation. Because it is tough out there. The world is tough. COVID has been tough. Everything's been tough. And to have a community that's willing to come together and support each other is amazing.'

A British cosplayer, Blake, talked about how the cosplay community can come together across national lines. They discussed going to a con in the United States and being able to easily flow into the cosplay community there because they had a shared knowledge as well as a shared cosplay language. They described how there was an awkwardness when first interacting, but as soon as they started discussing aspects of cosplay, the whole group fell together into a collective community.

For some cosplayers, the role of the community is what makes cosplay what it is. Riley, for example, when asked to explain what cosplay is for them, connected it intimately to the role of the community:

I guess cosplay is, like, where creativity and community meet, I think. You take a thing that can be quite, quite personal . . . And then you take it to a space where actually loads of other people are doing the same thing. And all of a sudden it's like, 'Are these people like me? I have – I have friends here. I have allies here. I have people who think and want to create in the same way that I do.'

The community, for Riley, is what makes cosplaying *cosplay* – and the community is united in the act of doing. The creativity of the personal act is what actually makes it communal, because the movement from the personal to the communal is highly experiential and deeply moving.

Both Mia and Bailey described how they got involved in cosplaying in groups. For many, friends will band together to do a group cosplay – each picking a character from the same show or movie. I previously discussed a group all cosplaying the main characters from Netflix's *She-Ra* – this is a group cosplay. Some people got into cosplay through this, needing to help out a group of friends by joining them in cosplay. For others, like Bailey, they used the group cosplay experience as a way of forcing themselves to cosplay different things, but also to make new friends in the cosplay experience.

But not all aspects of the cosplay community can be positive. Racism, misogyny, transphobia and other types of hate speech and action are still present. I (and cosplayers I spoke to) have seen white cosplayers doing blackface to fit a character of colour, for instance. Others complained to me about seeing someone wearing cultural dress incorrectly, such as Japanese kimonos and yukatas or Scottish kilts.

Racism also surfaces in the relationship with photographers. Many cosplayers of colour discussed having photographers ignore them while in groups or refuse to work with them simply because of their skin colour. The UK cosplay scene has recently been working to stop this, with more and more cosplayers of colour speaking out about poor behaviour from photographers and videographers who have treated them differently from their white counterparts. This can create more walls for cosplayers of colour to find entry points to the larger cosplay scene or to develop a following online. But more than that, it emphasizes the idea that cosplay is a predominantly white activity.

The more regional cosplay communities can also be riddled with cliques. One person discussed how their connections to publications and photographers made it difficult to make friends in the cosplay community. Many, they told me in confidence, had become friends with them but then immediately stopped when it became clear they were not going to easily get in touch with their connections. A lot of people wanted to use cosplayers with more followers on social media to try and create a space to become – potentially – a professional cosplayer. The desire for fame, and the way individuals can use their connections in the community, can therefore be an incredible asset to some, but can also be detrimental to the relationships built for others.

I found walls when it came to cliques as well – sometimes I was able to navigate through them during the course of this research, and some I found quite difficult. When attending MegaCon in Manchester, for example, I found myself completely ignored when trying to ask questions of the group helping to run the cosplay part of the con. I hadn't even had the time to introduce myself as a scholar – if I do this and then people ignore me, I chalk it up to not being interested in sharing their experiences with me, which doesn't bother me. But to be ignored before introducing myself, I found quite isolating. For any new cosplayer on the scene, I could imagine a similar experience would be so off-putting as to make them consider quitting.

In contrast, I was ushered past many cliques when attending CosXpo. At the beginning, I introduced myself to some photographers and by questioning them ended up being pushed around their various photoshoots throughout the day. Because of their openness, they introduced me to many cosplayers in the scene, all of whom knew each other and kept to the same circles of friends and experiences. It wasn't until I was speaking to another cosplayer who was not a part of this group that I realized my luck. They told me how difficult it can be to break into that clique of cosplayers and how newly coming to the community can be quite challenging.

This is an important part of doing anthropological research to note. The term 'gatekeepers' is used frequently by people who conduct fieldwork. Often, before going into a community, we have to reach out to certain people who can give us greater access. When studying a Christian Science church, for example, I had to contact the head of the church before attending, and their okay made other members of the church feel more comfortable speaking to me. This is also how it worked in the cosplay community, though the relationships are a little more complicated to figure out than for a very small singular church.

When it came to studying cosplay in the south of England, I had a stroke of luck. One of the first people I spoke to was a photographer who was well respected by many cosplayers. As he carried me from place to place introducing me to people, they felt comfortable chatting with me because I was considered okay by someone they trusted. This also happened after introducing myself to another prominent figure in the cosplay community in the south. After several months of interviewing, I discovered that some cosplayers specifically asked this person if I was safe to talk to and only agreed to an interview after I was approved.

This is typically how interviews are achieved for social scientists. After you interview a few people, they reach out to their friends to okay the process, which leads to more interviews, and this snowballs into a nice collection. The initial contacts who promote our research to their friends are called 'gatekeepers', as they are the gateway we move through to access the community. What happened with the cliques in Manchester was a demonstration of how lucky I had been finding the primary gatekeepers in my previous endeavours, rather than something particularly different about the Manchester group.

Let's take a moment now to consider the fact that, so far, I've been referring to the cosplay community as just that: a community. However, this includes individuals from very different backgrounds, whether socioeconomic, national, gender or otherwise. Can we, therefore, truly claim that the cosplay community is accurately described as a community? Obviously, the wonderful displays of togetherness described by Sam make one think of cosplay as a community. But we also have heard experiences of racism and other forms of bigotry. As an anthropologist, I have to consider what a community is in terms of the discipline, and to what else those who cosplay may be referred.

Let's put 'community' to the side for now and start with another word often used to talk about cosplay: 'subculture'. Many groups in pop culture more generally are described as subcultures; this is because they are seen as both distinguished from but embedded within a larger group. Dick Hebdige is perhaps the most prominent scholar who laid the foundations of the study of sub-culture, through his focused study of youth subcultures in Britain. For Hebdige, subcultures are formed to challenge dominant the ideologies and social normalization that occur in the wider cul-ture. Therefore, their style and interactions are all done as acts of resistance.[1]

While cosplay may not necessarily be embedded in the every-day actions of wider society, and it can definitely be a form of resistance and subversion, it is not always like this. The wider cul-tural group, of course, can also be vastly different in different areas of the world and yet participants see themselves in cosplayers from a variety of locations, as described by my participant Blake, who found community in cosplayers even when in a different country or culture.

Hebdige also commented on how the style of subcultures becomes gently folded into the mainstream society it initially fought to separate itself from. This was evident in punk. What first was radical, and sometimes a source of fear for the mainstream culture, slowly became more commodified until its presence was a part of the mainstream.[2] The commodification and the folding in of cosplay into wider mainstream culture has been occurring in the past ten to twenty years. Since cosplay was described and coined by Takahashi, its popularity has risen rapidly. The emergence of pro-fessional cosplayers demonstrates its growing commodification. However, I don't think cosplayers were ever viewed with fear. In fact, mainstream society at worst saw them as social losers rather than punkish miscreants.

Another primary critique of the term 'subculture' is that the concepts of both subculture and culture are too rigid. They are not thought of as fluid groups who can shift and move, but rather as static elements that either are incorporated or stand in contrast. People, and the groups of people which make up communities and societies, are more fluid.

A more complicated term which has a growing presence in discussions about cosplay and other nerd subgroups is the 'neo-tribe'. The concept of the neo-tribe is primarily based on the work of Michel Maffesoli, a French sociologist. Building on the idea of modern society's push towards more and more individualization, Maffesoli believed that, in response, individuals would start to embrace nostalgia, bringing in an era of neo-tribalism.[3] This is starting to take us quite far from the world of cosplay, but the basic idea is that modernity causes social fragmentation. We no longer live in close-knit familial groups. The person who grew up surrounded by family in rural Kentucky, for example, now moves to New York City, separating themselves from the world of 'community' as we once knew it.

The preference towards neo-tribes is twofold. The first is the growing importance of 'found family' in popular culture and discourse – the idea that an individual is not bound to their birth family, but rather can build their own family from those around them. The second preference is the idea that concepts like 'culture', and therefore 'subculture', are inherently rigid. Neo-tribes, by contrast, are more ambivalent, reflecting a state of mind or a lifestyle choice, rather than as strongly cemented as, say, familial clan-based organizations or formalized nationalities.[4]

The primary advantage of neo-tribalism is how it sits in contrast to the idea of a subculture. This is getting into the definition wars undertaken by academics the world over. But in order to take on a definition, one must think about everything which underlies it. For example, if we disagree with the concept of a wider semi-homogenous culture, then the idea of a subculture, which is a part of this wider culture, wouldn't really work for us. Similarly, neo-tribalism's reliance on the way modernity has impacted individuals, and its assumptions about how people functioned prior to this in community groups, is something to consider.

I'm not going to get into complicated arguments about modernity because they take us way more off track than we already are, and would probably fall far more into the boring camp than discussing fun cosplays. However, I do disagree with a lot of the underlying axioms of Maffesoli's concept, including both of these facets: how societies worked prior to industrialization, and why people are choosing found families in the first place. One aspect, for example, that Maffesoli does not consider is when the home group

Father and son cosplaying together at Stars of Time 2023, Weston-super-Mare.

purposefully ostracizes individuals, which leads them to their found family, as is often the case for members of the LGBT+ community.

During the course of my research, while chatting with cosplayers, the term 'community' was used freely. (Only academics sit around overthinking the terms we are using and why they may or may not matter.) However, I don't think the individuals talking about the cosplay community are that far off. The idea of a community, sociologically speaking, is basically a group of people who have something in common. For example, this can be the location where they live: if I live in Brooklyn, I'm a part of the Brooklyn community, for example; if I move away from Brooklyn, I'm no longer part of the Brooklyn community. I may feel some affinity, and I may be able to share some of the same language if I run into someone else who still is a part of that community, but ultimately I'm no longer there and therefore don't belong. Communities are built on this – the in-group versus the out-group. To have a community, you must have people who belong. And one of the consequences of having people who belong is you have people who don't.

But like the idea of neo-tribes, communities can be fluid. Albert Hirschmann, for example, wrote about 'shifting involvements' in communities. People can vary their involvement in their community and can even drop in and out of their 'belong' status depending on the individual. As Hirschmann pointed out, this is most common in groups which require some degree of active engagement from its members.[5] If to be in the cosplay community you must cosplay, then individuals may feel themselves dropping in and out of the community depending on how much energy they have to give to keep their involvement active. One individual I spoke to was a student who felt they had little time or money to engage with cosplay. They still considered themselves a cosplayer but admitted to no longer feeling as 'connected'.

Similarly, we have to really think about the experience of Blake, who felt they belong to the cosplay community and felt an equal sense of belonging in a new place among new people. While Benedict Anderson's work was initially set to explain ideas of nations, his concept of 'imagined communities' (discussed in the previous chapter) can help here. Anderson talked about how people can feel as if they share with other members of their community, even if they have never actually met them.[6] Cosplayers can share a sense of community with another cosplayer, even if they are somewhere very different and the two have never met in person. Here, I should stress, Anderson does not mean 'imagined' as in 'not real'. These communities are very real, especially to the individuals who belong to them. What he means by 'imagined' is that it relies on a kind of group socio-cognitive element, a shared sense of imagination of what it *means* to belong.

Anderson describes how important the role of media is in the development of imagined communities, and I think this is equally important to the development of cosplay as a community. Social media has allowed many individuals from around the world to share in a collective experience of the idea of cosplay; in an instant people are able to understand both what it means to do cosplay and what it means to be a cosplayer. The development of how-to books and videos from creators also allows the group a shared experience of skill growth, which contributes to the sense of community.

All this digression is included to share what we mean when we talk about the cosplay community. It is one where individuals may drop in and out, as well as contribute to a varying degree throughout their life. But it is also one individuals see as necessary to contribute to – in other words, in order to belong to the cosplay community, one must cosplay.

Photographers I spoke to discussed with me this aspect of the cosplay community. One shared how they used to cosplay, but fell out of it when they felt they weren't as skilled as their friends. So instead, they began to take photos of cosplayers and found a talent for it. They expressed to me that they are still somehow a part of the development of the cosplay community and its media and culture, but also not technically a member of the community. They live in a limbo state – seeing and experiencing some of the aspects of the 'belonging' crowd, while not actually really belonging anymore. But one of the greatest benefits of the cosplay community, for those who are within the 'in' group of belonging, is that one can find community among anyone who cosplays. One of the wonderful things about cosplayers is that they find themselves bound together through their act of doing and their performance of creativity.

While there are issues in the cosplay community such as racism and ableism, it is important to keep in mind that cosplay is simply reflecting the wider culture. Nevertheless, there are active movements within the community to enact direct change through sharing experiences and communicating with one another, creating greater lines of strength and growth for the wider group.

One of the unifying factors among cosplayers is their relationship to media, performance and skill. As fans of the same media forms, they can connect to their mythological narratives and find similar values even across regional or national boundaries. We have already talked about how performance is enacted among cosplayers. But cosplayers are also a community built on shared knowledge and experience. They are a skilful community of creativity, born from the beautiful act of dressing up.

6

Skill and Cosplay

A crucial question which faces every beginner cosplayer is the all-important 'How do I even do this?' When I was making small talk with new cosplayers, this was a constant fear. People expressed concern over not having a sewing machine or having a hand-me-down one from a parent which they had never touched. One person admitted to needing to blow off dust from their machine before realizing they didn't even know how to turn it on. Others said they were too busy to dedicate time to lengthy classes on sewing when they only cared about creating the one or two things they needed for their costume.

The cosplay community is often defined – by those both inside and outside – by its relationship to skill. As we have already discussed, my participant Riley did this, describing cosplay as 'where creativity and community meet'. The development of creativity is what defines cosplay for Riley, and creativity means developing skill. For Riley, I'm sure sewing ability is not important to whether they are 'successful' at cosplaying, but their creativity and involvement in the community mean the skills associated with creativity are constantly being cultivated. Avery also emphasized creativity and the development of skill. When asked what cosplay is for them, Avery stressed three things: creativity, having fun and how cosplay helps their mental health. When discussing the creativity of cosplay, Avery talked about not only costume creation, but learning different related skills, and even mentioned a desire to learn blacksmithing.

More seasoned cosplayers always have the same advice: you learn to cosplay by doing it. Essentially, the skill involved in both starting and continuing cosplay is the simple act of doing. There are how-to books associated with it, and other courses both online and offline, such as tutorials on YouTube, magazines with light instructions such as the *Cosplay Journal* and even sewing patterns from major producers like McCalls. However, these are presented to cosplayers as sources to start the process and learn from it: the pattern is meant to be cut and constructed; the information in the book, tutorial and journal are instructions to guide an individual in the act of creating.

Cosplayers learn through the process of doing and exploring their doing with others. While at a con, a conversation I was having with one cosplayer was interrupted by another coming up to chat. This new cosplayer excitedly showed their sleeve to my cosplayer participant, explaining how they had hand-embroidered the flowers on it. The two then launched into conversation about exactly how they did it, how long it took and how many times the creator had to take out stitches and try again.

Riley talked about their progression creating costumes by stating they enjoy the process more than they initially thought they would: 'When I started, it was a lot of, like, buying and altering. Which I think helps because if I'd have just tried to jump straight in with just making things from scratch, I don't think I would have ever progressed past one.' Riley started with one aspect of skill and grew, over time and through the process of doing, into making full costumes from scratch.

Booth of cosplay books and resources at MCM London 2022.

Sewing patterns for sale at MCM London 2022.

Gísli Pálsson discussed the idea of 'enskilment', where knowledge is not always a cognitive experience, but rather can be bodily. Pálsson explained how enskilment is a type of immersion in the world, a way of learning encapsulated by the simple act of being deeply involved in the flow of the everyday, rather than acquiring knowledge through a cognitive process. In other words, learning is something people do actively through living in the world.[1] One way of understanding enskilment is through processes of social knowledge. Someone who is described as being 'street smart', for example, has knowledge not found in books or able to be quizzed; rather it is learned through the simple act of experiencing life.

Cosplay learning is often a combination of these two types of approaches. Assuming one can learn everything about being a 'good' cosplayer from simply reading books about costume construction does not take into account the more lived idea of communal creation and storytelling, the bodily performance of modelling the costume or the way a cosplayer chooses the costume they are to embody in the first place. Being an incredibly skilled sewer does not necessarily always translate to being an incredibly skilled cosplayer, nor is the opposite true. Cosplay is a communal learning activity, one in which the community comes together to actively share their experiences and costumes so others may learn from them, whether this be through learning new techniques or seeing the world of cosplay in a slightly different way than the cosplayer initially conceived.

That being said, this does predicate a certain type of skill in the conversation. So far, we've talked about skill as a form of costume construction or in sewing. Skill comes down to how the costume is actually put together, how good the sewing is and how accurately the costume represents the original character chosen to be cosplayed. This isn't always the skill cosplayers seek, though. Some do not necessarily want to perfectly replicate costumes. Sometimes, it is easier to construct a costume that is not an exact replica. While talking with me, Charlie explained how they would carefully study the costume of the original character in order to decide which pieces were necessary to make and which weren't. In this way, they are able to construct a similar costume to the original – where the audience understands who is being cosplayed – but with less effort.

Other cosplayers purposefully alter costumes for a variety of reasons. Most often these changes are to adjust the costume to better fit the cosplayer's body. Sometimes, this is for comfort: the cosplayer understands what is most comfortable on their body and shifts the costume to accommodate this. In other instances, cosplayers change the costume to fit their bodies in a more dynamic way. Riley, for example, talked about making a cosplay of a female Austin Powers to fit a female body. In these instances, cosplayers actively change the costume in order to better understand their own gendered bodies.

Some cosplayers of colour also actively change the costume to fit their bodies, particularly when it comes to hair choices. Some Black cosplayers decide to wear more natural hair, such as choosing a large blonde afro instead of the character's original straight blonde hair. These changes reflect the cosplayer's body and the way their hair is naturally without making it difficult for audience members to recognize the original character.

These active choices are also a type of skill. It requires skill to recognize aspects of the costume which define the character and which are less important. Sociologist Erving Goffman had a term for this: 'identity kits'.[2] Identity kits refer to the aspects of a person's appearance which mark them and their identity, the parts which make them recognizably *them*. This isn't just for fictional characters, but for all of us. We all have aspects of our appearance which can be replicated for the purposes of identity replication. Because our clothing represents who we are and our identity, as discussed in Chapter Two, our identity kits are things marked on our bodies that represent identities, whether a fictional character or a physical person.

While there is skill involved in costume construction when making one from scratch, there are other forms of skill involved as well. Not all cosplayers sew their own costumes. In fact, many purchase them, both those which are widely produced and those which are commissioned. There is another skill involved in buying costumes. Some cosplayers make small alterations to purchased costumes in order to make sure it fits just as well as if they had made it themselves, but for the rest, care is required to ensure the costume fits them well. There is also skill involved in quality checking costumes before purchase, especially if buying online. Cosplayers share knowledge of certain sources and acquire a skill in knowing where to go, or who to commission, to ensure their costume is what they want and what they expect.

It should be stressed that the ability to make your own costume is typically a privilege in regards to both money and resources. While purchased costumes can also be expensive, larger items for costume construction, such as a sewing machine and regular access to materials like fabric, are not economically feasible for many cosplayers. The domestic space necessary, even at its minimum, to make costumes also costs money in rent or a mortgage, which not all cosplayers can afford. Emma lives in just one room as they are currently at university. 'My bedroom is really tiny,' they said,

Section of the craft room of cosplayer 'Olly Rose (@ lilistprince).

and I could see the whole space from the Zoom call screen. 'I just don't have the money and the resources to be buying material and everything.'

Whether the cosplayer is creating their costume from scratch or purchasing it, the necessary skill is not accumulated alone, but often through their relationship to both the craft and other cosplayers. On different social media sites, cosplayers not only show off their costumes to other cosplayers, but ask questions and get advice on the process behind the costume. Elliot, for example, said they

Makeup tutorial by Begonia Fernandez Martin of BBSFX at CosXpo 2022.

Sample prosthetics used in both SFX makeup and cosplay.

primarily use social media to follow other cosplayers, but stressed that they prefer following individuals they feel they can learn from.

Sometimes knowledge is also shared at cons. This can be in personal communication, as it was for the two cosplayers discussing hand-embroidering stitches on a sleeve, or it can be more formal. At several events, performance stages are taken over with people teaching sewing skills, prosthetics and special effects make-up or wig styling.

Some of the skills cosplayers possess can be difficult to explain directly or clearly. They may not necessarily be craft skills, like the ability to sew a straight hem, but more complicated concepts, like picking the right character or figuring out which aspects of the costume can be neglected in the construction while still maintaining an appearance of perfection. When talking to cosplayers, I found that sometimes they struggled to communicate their process in these aspects of cosplay. It was all something more 'felt' than 'learned'. When it comes to skill in costume choice, Elliot tried to explain how a cosplayer needs to have individual knowledge of another person in order to properly choose a character for them:

> I mean, mostly with my best friend it makes sense. Because I've known her for so long, I'm just kind of like, 'Yeah, you're a gremlin. Go off and do your cosplay.' But sometimes, my boyfriend just kind of comes up with, like, cosplay ideas. He's never cosplayed before. But he wants to get into it. And so sometimes he comes up with some ideas where I'm like, 'No, you should never do that.' So sometimes if I know the person enough, I'll be – I'll be like, you know what, you stick with that.

'Olly Rose (@lilistprince) as BB8 from the *Star Wars* franchise.

David Barber (Barbᴅwitt Cosplay) as Cad Bane at CosXpo 2023.

Cosplayer @ex.shadow as Ganondorf from *The Legend of Zelda*.

Cosplayer @kirahmiya as the Pokémon Mimikyu.

Cosplayer @chocoblowcosplay as Giorno at CosXpo 2023.

An example of a larger cosplay build: Spirit Walker UK at CosXpo 2023.

Cosplayers (@normie.ik and @rb._99) at MCM London 2023.

Group cosplay (@cosmiicdolly, @rowanix and @cooliogoolio) of
The Owl House at MCM London 2023.

Myself in cosplay as Chise Hatori from *The Ancient Magus' Bride*.

'Olly Rose (@lilistprince) as Moist from *Discworld*.

Katie (@katiedoescosplay) as Gandalf from *The Lord of the Rings*.

Cosplayer @cosplayshino as Yor from *Spy × Family*.

Cosplayer @seren_gaeaf as Melania from *Elden Ring*, a character typically portrayed as revealing/naked, complicating the idea of 'sexy' cosplay.

Cosplayer @katyafern as Lust.

Pidge (@cospidgey) as Mohg, Lord of Blood, from *Elden Ring*.

Lukey P as a steampunk plague doctor.

Cosplayer @supersailorjunko as a chain-chomp
from the *Super Mario* series.

What Elliot demonstrates is that not only do cosplayers have a skill in figuring out which characters fit them, they also have an ability to decide which characters suit other cosplayers around them. This is another example of enskilment, a process of social learning acquired through simply doing. For those first coming into cosplay, a lack of this skill can feel overwhelming. Online groups have many people posting photos of themselves and asking for advice on which character to cosplay.

When we talk about the skill involved in cosplay, sewing construction is definitely important, but it is by far not the only one or the most prevalent. These more quiet skills – harnessed and honed through doing, performing and being around cosplayers – are important aspects of both the development of skill and the cosplay community.

These skills can only be acquired through the process of doing, failing and reconsidering. My own cosplay had snags that I would have been able to avoid with more experience. The character wears a simple outfit, which was, admittedly, one of the reasons I picked her. I knew I had, at the time, no skill in clothing construction (I have since started teaching myself to sew). Instead of creating a costume, or even buying one, I decided instead to purchase clothes from charity shops and thrift stores which fit the general look of the costume I was after. I considered this a good mixture between the two worlds of buying and making – a type of makeshifting.

It was not the makeshifting that was a problem, but rather my discomfort in different clothes. I'm a jeans and T-shirt kind of girl, and therefore was unaccustomed to wearing skirts. When I do, it's typically when it's a little colder out, so I'm wearing tights or leggings underneath. When I wore my cosplay to a con, though, I found myself incredibly uncomfortable. I was intensely aware of the fact that I was wearing a skirt. I was conscious of how I had to sit or move or stand in a way I hadn't been accustomed to really thinking about before. And over time, the discomfort grew from mental to physical as I wasn't prepared for the way my thighs would be affected by the difference between wearing a skirt and trousers.

When I later talked of my experiences with cosplayers, they all understood exactly what I was saying. One told me that was why they never cosplayed in skirts. Another admonished me for not knowing I had to wear something under my skirt. A cosplayer shared with me that their first few cosplays carried the same issues, both the physical pain of not knowing about certain clothing items as well as the discomfort I faced at the beginning. It was all about learning how to move in different clothes as well as which clothes suit you – not to be attractive, but to be comfortable.

What I experienced was what Umberto Eco calls epidermic self-awareness. Eco wrote about the feeling when wearing jeans which were still too tight after losing some weight. He was incredibly aware of how the jeans felt on his body, how they pinched and restricted movement: 'As a result, I lived in the knowledge that I had jeans on, whereas normally we live forgetting that we're wearing undershorts or trousers.'[3] Epidermic self-awareness refers to when something we are wearing encroaches on our bodily experiences and makes us aware of the 'edges' – the limits and boundaries of our body. We become incredibly aware of where our body ends and the clothes begin.

Cosplayers told me of their experiences with epidermic self-awareness, but always as an explanation that something was wrong with the cosplay choice to begin with. My own character choice may have been wrong – I was not as attuned to my character and therefore not as comfortable in the performed skin, which should be as comfortable as my own. If the character was not wrong, then my interpretation was. Like the cosplayer who never wears skirts, I could have found another way of portraying the character that more easily combined myself and my character into one being and experience. In fact, in a future con, I did make small alterations which helped with the physical discomfort – wearing skin-coloured tights to mimic the idea of bare legs while still understanding my own comfort level, for example. At my photoshoot for the images in this book, I wore black tights instead of nude tights. Primarily this was because I hadn't bought nude tights yet, but more generally it was cold and I wanted to be more comfortable while walking around the nearby woodland paths. However, I also considered the original character, as there are several scenes in the show where she wears black leggings or tights.

These are not failings I could have known prior to my experience, I should stress. These are issues almost all the cosplayers I encountered also had at one time. They told me of costumes they made that felt immensely uncomfortable when wearing and of pieces they slaved over that they discarded almost immediately after finishing. They described cosplays they made, wore and never returned to again. These issues of epidermic self-awareness are not unique to new cosplayers, but the ability to understand what went wrong and how to potentially keep it from happening again is all learned by doing, and is felt innately by more experienced cosplayers.

One place where a cosplayer's skill is ultimately put to the test is in masquerades and competitions. These typically take place at fan conventions, often at the end of the day. Exactly how they are defined and therefore actualized for the stage can be different depending on the con, but generally masquerades are non-judged and involve cosplayers simply posing to music. Competitions, on the other hand, are often restricted to cosplayers who have handmade their costume, and can involve music and/or full skits in the performance of the character. In both, there are two skills: the quality of the costume and the performance of the character.

For some competitions, entrants need to have their costumes inspected by judges prior to the event, so they can ask questions about the construction to ensure only those actually made by the individuals are being shown. One participant told me that while judging for a competition, they thought a costume had been bought but the cosplayer proved that it was constructed by showing pictures of their process.

The performance part of the competition can be simply poses set to music or an entire skit, depending on the cosplayer's own interests as well as the competition in question.

Different organizers can have different preferences between these two aspects of the competition, which can at times also be different from what the audience may want. At one competition, the winner was cosplaying a character from *West World*. They had constructed the entire outfit, including building a corset, for their cosplay. Despite this high level of skill, the audience felt an armour build should have won because of both the performance and the skill involved.

There are often disagreements in the cosplay community about the types of skills involved. In my conversation with Charlie, for example, they started by saying what matters most is skill in construction and whether the costume on its own best represents the character. They focused a lot on the accuracy of the

Cosplayer on stage at CosXpo 2022.

costume, and the way the costume is constructed, though they did acknowledge that 'if you've got the money to make it as accurate as possible, and resources, it's going to be better.' However, when asked what the difference was for them between cosplay and just 'dressing up', they said it had to be the whole combination of costume and play: 'So when you cosplay . . . you're in the costume for that person. And to me, that then means that you take on a little bit of their persona, and you're acting the way that they would.' Comparing it to Halloween, when many people dress as characters or figures from popular culture, Charlie said Halloween is an example of 'just dressing up': 'To my mind, cosplay is essentially like an actor going on stage in full costume. And you know . . . your character . . . they do this, that and the other. So cosplay, for me, is taking on the persona of that character.' Therefore, the importance of the skill in construction was overtaken by the skill in performance during the conversation. Different cosplayers can privilege different aspects, and these can change depending on the time or event.

Music choice for the performance is also important and directly relates to the character. Although they do not typically enter competitions, Riley talked about how they put together playlists of music associated with a cosplay when they are doing a photoshoot. The music could involve the soundtrack of the original media but could also be other music like pop songs or jazz which resonates with the character they are constructing and performing. Like other acts of enskilment, the process of listening to a playlist while doing a performance photoshoot was something Riley learned while interacting with others. They saw someone else doing it, and how they were able to be 'in the zone'. Seeing its success, they started trying it for themselves. The music choice for the competition performance is incredibly important to the performance. It helps to demonstrate to the audience and the judges how the cosplayer understands their character, and to communicate their performance even to audience members far away from the stage. So in many ways, the skill in cosplay is not just in the construction of costume, but also in the choice of music, the ability to perform and even in the choice of character in the first place.

The role of the audience in the competition is incredibly important. During one competition I watched, a group in the audience excitedly whooped for a performer and I assumed they were friends with the cosplayer. However, they continued to be excitedly interactive with each performer, clapping along to some music and giving big whoops and applause to characters they recognized and loved. The emcee began to interact with this group a bit more, and cosplayers actively used their energy to fuel the performance, moving more excitedly when the clapping started or bowing in their direction when it was a character they enjoyed.

Competitions, however, also display some of the discrepancies in the cosplay community, and help to perpetuate some of the issues cosplayers fight against for those who are looking to be a part of it. The most notable is that cosplayers do not always make their own costumes. In fact, one person I spoke to said that it was the most expensive costume they had ever bought, as they don't have time to devote to crafting their own. The costume was expensive because it had been custom made, and the props commissioned from a local artist. While some may see this cosplayer as lacking skill in construction, they regularly demonstrated skill in the modelled performance of their characters, the choices they made about which character they would cosplay and even knowing the right person to contact to make the costume for them.

For my own cosplay, I lacked the skill to make a costume, so instead I chose to do the same as Riley when they started: buy clothes and alter them. I pieced together my outfit from charity shops. My prop, however, was made by my husband, who is adept at woodworking. I found there was a skill in trying to match the original, but knew some alterations would need to be made either by me or in my portrayal of the character. It was important, for example, to get a jacket which did not fit me because the character's jacket was big on her.

Some elements of cosplay construction can skew more towards white people, making things more complicated for Black cosplayers. One Black cosplayer told me how most wig tutorials demonstrate how to put wigs over white hair, not Black hair. They had to learn simply by doing in order to figure out how to use wigs for themselves. Another cosplayer told me body paint make-up is often made with white skin in mind. When wanting to cosplay as an alien figure from *Star Wars* who had green skin, for example, this cosplayer would have to put on body make-up that made them white and then apply the coloured body paint. Essentially, Black cosplayers often faced extra hurdles in their construction in order to be considered on a par with white cosplayers, which added both more time and more money.

As much as cosplay competitions and masquerades are meant just to be fun, the competition angle can often cause anxiety and worry. Elliot, for instance, said they wanted to partake but didn't feel they had the necessary skills. 'I just don't feel like I'm at the right level yet,' is how Elliot put it, shifting slightly in their seat as they talked about it. 'And then I just . . . I've never felt like any of them have particularly been so good that I should show them off to everyone.'

The conversation around competitions also opens up the argument around elitism in cosplay. Elitism is a highly contested debate in the cosplay community, with many people having different opinions on the matter. Most of it centres around the idea that competitions are only for those who have hand crafted their costumes, and there is no equivalent for individuals who have not. Those who argue that competitions are inherently elitist stress the emphasis on accuracy and how it supports the financial barriers impacting some people. Arthur pointed out how focus on the need for accuracy above all else has made cosplay elitist: 'Now [cosplay] is something that – it's becoming more well known. This has caused a lot of people to come and a lot of elitism, a lot of barriers, a lot of accuracy you must plan, otherwise you're not supposed to do it . . . it wasn't so much a thing when I started.' This means cosplayers who like to put their own spin on the costume, either for personal identity, personal safety or personal preference, are often considered not as 'good' at cosplay as white, thin, able-bodied cosplayers who can represent the characters bodily. Accuracy at competitions has then extended off the stage and cosplayers who make alterations are made to feel inferior by others who establish the competition standards more generally.

Bailey also noted how a lot of the conversation around cosplay centres on the need to make it yourself, above anything else. 'I've made costumes, and I have hated every second of being in them,' they said. 'That's a bad costume.' Here, Bailey is emphasizing the 'play' side of cosplay, stressing that having fun and feeling good in the costume should be more important than how one came to possess it in the first place – just as Avery does in their description of cosplay as needing to be fun.

That being said, some cosplayers I spoke to defended competitions. Blake, for example, enjoyed the process of making costumes and saw cosplay competitions as the primary place for them to be able to show off their skill. They said that instead of removing competitions, there should be more spaces for all kinds of cosplay to thrive. Some cons are already making room for different kinds of competitions. Sci-fi Scarborough in 2023 had different competition categories depending on a variety of factors, including both age and way the costume was put together. Handmade costumes competed only against handmade costumes, and store-bought competed against store-bought, but both had a place.

The conversation around the skill involved in cosplay also needs to include the development of the professional cosplayer. For some, cosplay has become their life in a different way – they are able to make a financial living through their art. Cosplayers such as Maul Cosplay, Yaya Han or Kamui Cosplay have been able to carve out a space in which they are able to communicate cosplay regularly. The growth of professional cosplayers also means a large number of amateurs are constantly seeking to reach the status of professional. But what is the difference between an amateur and a professional?

One thing should be noted: there are very few, if any, cosplayers who are able to make a living exclusively doing cosplay and nothing else. Even the professional cosplayers mentioned above do other things. Jessica Nigri and Meg Turney, for example, also make money modelling in other scenarios such as magazines or on their personal Only Fans account. Kamui Cosplay sells costume construction patterns and also makes costumes for television and film.

Some write for the cosplay community, such as Holly Swinyard – who probably would not describe themself as a professional cosplayer – who has carved out a space in the community as a pop culture writer, editing the *Cosplay Journal* and writing books about the history of cosplay and the construction of costume.

That being said, there is a certain level of expectation relating to the skill involved in costume construction for professional cosplayers. Although one person I spoke to said the only difference between an amateur and a professional is the exchange of money, others noted that professionals demonstrate more skill in the construction and wearing of their costumes. Charlie, for example, said that aside from time and money, the primary difference is in costume accuracy. They then went into a full explanation of different types of costumes if they were making something from *The Lord of the Rings*. Doing a simple cloak with the proper colours would still be a good cosplay, but a professional would probably go into the minute details of the costume. All of this, they noted, did take time and money, but professionals probably have more resources to spend on these details.

How professionals achieve this skill, however, was even more contested. Some, for example, argued that they became professional because of their skill level, and the reception of audiences to their cosplays was central. Others, however, saw it along different lines. One cosplayer believed many professionals got there through other means, primarily their prevalence on social media. This meant they received more attention and funds for the builds of their cosplays, which caused them to appear more skilful even if they weren't. Stevie focused on a professional's talent, as well as expressing how some professionals offer different aspects of themselves and their art to the community.

One cosplayer I interviewed, Avery, was what I would consider a professional. Their job was to cosplay, and they made a good amount of money doing it. However, when I asked Avery if they considered themself a professional, they giggled and said, 'No, absolutely not.' When I pressed on why, they said their costume isn't always handmade and they don't tend to care about make-up. They continued that they tend to be 'not as serious' as other professionals.

There is, typically, a perceived skewing of professional cosplayers who primarily identify as female. I say typically because, as mentioned above, many professional cosplayers do other things for money and therefore it can be difficult to determine who is considered a 'professional' by others. That being said, the most visually recognized professional cosplayers tend to be women who also model. People like Jessica Nigri and Meg Turney, for example, are well known for making cosplays which feminize characters, and sometimes also sexualize them, a conversation for the next chapter.

Skill is often discussed when it comes to cosplay, but there are a variety of skills that go into it: from costume construction to wig styling to make-up, and even choosing which character to pick in the first place. Much of the way cosplayers learn and hone their skill is through the community – conversations with other cosplayers as well as tutorials both in person at cons and online. But, most importantly, people learn through cosplaying. The art of actually doing cosplay is the best process of learning, and many cosplayers express glee at their mess-ups early on and how they have grown and learned from them.

Tinufel Cosplay
as Princess Zelda
at MCM London
2023.

The express focus on skill, however, also means that there can be elitism in cosplay and the community. While some may see it as a positive joyful celebration of what the cosplay community is capable of, others see it as a wall which means only certain types of cosplay receive attention, specifically those which are 'accurate' to the original character, from costume to body. It also presents financial difficulties for some to overcome.

Kim as Tom Nook at MCM London 2023.

The rise of the professional cosplayer is particularly interesting. It demonstrates the impact cosplay can have in society and how cosplay has captured the wider imagination. There is enough interest in cosplay to present opportunities for individuals to make a living doing it. However, a lot of professional cosplayers stress this elitism: costumes must be made, and specific body types are privileged over others. The dominance of female professional cosplayers, as well as the emphasis on certain body types, are important to keep in mind when we think about the role of gender and sexuality in cosplay as well.

7

Cosplay, Gender and Sexuality

On a cursory look through social media hashtags involving cosplay, you would think the only participants are female. Part of the reason is the role of female professional cosplayers. Because professionals are very prolific on social media, they conquer the online sphere and are typically the first form of cosplay others see before getting further into the community. In particular, female professional cosplayers who also sexualize their characters seem the most prevalent, simply through larger engagement with these types of cosplayers from those outside of it. There has been a growth in sexualization of cosplay more generally. Many porn sites have a cosplay section for those interested.

In this chapter, we're going to explore these two dynamics of cosplay: gender and sexuality. Cosplay can play an important role in the discussion around gender. We've mentioned before how people can choose whether they are going to cosplay the character as their own gender or as a different one. 'Crossplay' is the term sometimes used for cosplaying a character who is a different gender to your own, a reference to the idea of cross-dressing. However, some cosplayers dislike the term because of the complicated and problematic relationship between the concept of cross-dressing and the reality of trans lives. Because of this, throughout the rest of this book, I will be referring to 'crossplay' as drag cosplay, where the performer's gendered identity is different from that of the character they are playing. Despite my use of the word 'drag' here, those who do play a different gender tend not to see it as a gendered performance in the same way a drag performer might, but rather as a character performance. They are embodying the character as they are, rather than transforming the character.

Gender-bending cosplay is another way to manipulate conceptions of gender. In gender-bent cosplays, they transform the gender of their characters. While drag cosplay involves performing the character's gender when it is different from your own, most gender-bent cosplays transform the character's gender to fit the cosplayer's. Most often, this involves canonically male characters being performed as female. In both these cases, a transformation of gender is occurring: for the first, it's the cosplayer whose gendered identity changes; for the second, it's the character's. In either case, the performance of gender is taken into consideration, as well as what it means for a gender to be transformed in the first place.

Most of the cosplayers I spoke to who partook in drag cosplay did not think of their performance as being akin to or a subset of drag, but rather simply as a cosplay and nothing else. However, despite this, they were able to comment on the flexibility of gender as a concept to explain what they were doing. For example, Sam gushed in excitement at the idea of doing drag cosplays, especially in helping others to do them as well. In fact, Sam explained that because they're non-binary, all cosplay to them is a form of drag cosplay. This is slightly different to how non-binary cosplayer Holly Swinyard feels about cosplay. In a podcast interview, Holly said every character they cosplay is non-binary simply because Holly is the one doing it.[1]

Bailey also talked about how their cosplays, and their feelings about the cosplays, fluctuated based on their own feelings regarding their non-binary body:

> My gender expression can have, like, switches, and I kind of need to have backup plans and things because I'll be working on something, it'll be beautiful, lovely feminine dress. And then I'll be like the week before the call and working on it in floods of tears. I don't want to put this on, I don't want to put this on, I don't want to put this on. It's too girly. It's too femme. I don't want – I don't want that on my body.

In each of these instances, the cosplayer's own gender can either assist or completely conflict with their cosplays. It all comes down to the relationship the cosplayer has with their own body, as well as the social worlds they are about to move within.

Charlie commented that they often do male-based cosplays, which is not Charlie's own gender, primarily because they don't like wearing skirts. When I asked if, therefore, they would consider cosplaying a woman if she wore trousers, Charlie responded 'Yeah!' and went on to describe how they had even altered a female outfit which was supposed to be a skirt to look like a skirt, but really was constructed to be trousers so Charlie would feel more comfortable. But they tended to gravitate towards male characters anyway.

Others expressed a lack of interest in the gender when choosing a character. Emma tended to gravitate to female characters, but also commented that their favourite cosplay had been a male character. 'I think I prefer cosplaying the girls,' Emma said thoughtfully, 'but I don't think I pay attention to the gender. I think [their male character cosplay] felt like the character and I'm like, "Yes, I'm gonna cosplay this character."' When it comes to the performance part of the drag cosplay, Emma commented that it was bound to feel different when planning another gender. 'I know this might sound really weird,' they said (Emma typically warned me of elements before they spoke), 'but because I'm cosplaying as a guy, I kind of feel like a guy.'

As fashion writer Elizabeth Wilson stated in 1986, fashion is 'obsessed with gender'.[2] Even when we remove the cosplay aspect, clothes always have something to say about gender. Fashion sets out commentaries through images and has often been associated with conversations about power dynamics such as class divisions, racial differences and gender boundaries. Joanne Entwistle also points this out in their summary of how different anthropologists and sociologists have approached the topic of fashion over the years.[3]

When cosplayers create costumes, they are, by proxy, engaging with discourses involved in fashion. Bailey's discomfort with certain feminine or masculine looks when they, in that moment, do not feel feminine or masculine reflects the way fashion – including the costumes which are designed for characters – embodies and reinforces conceptions of gendered identities which can be read through clothes.

Judith Butler discussed the way gender is read and understood socially in our presentations of our selves in the ways we move, speak and dress. Butler started her approach to the study of gendered performance by first looking at linguistics, specifically linguistic performativity. Most performatives, she says, are statements which also perform a certain action and have a binding power in them. She specifically focused on aspects of performative speech at ceremonies. The power of the words 'I do' at weddings, for example, is a lot more than just a set of words – they are said in conjunction with a performance (the wedding) and also have a binding power in them (binding the speaker to the receiver in matrimony). Legal proceedings are similar. Words typically reserved for courtroom proceedings then spoken outside of the courtroom by people who are not judges do not have the same power as when they are spoken in the performance of the trial by the people who provide the binding power of the words. Essentially, Butler points out the power of words when paired with actions, particularly those which are culturally repetitive. The power of the wedding 'I do', for example, is only recognized because of the cultural repetition of what a wedding looks and sounds like.

Butler starts with the idea of linguistic performativity, and considers what this tells us about gender and the performance of gender. She says there is no inherent meaning to the word 'girl', in the same way there is no inherent meaning in 'I do' until it is demonstrated to be culturally important in its repetition. In other words, without the repetition of what it means to be 'girly' or have 'girlness', there isn't really anything inherently 'girl' about 'girl'. The idea of what is feminine is not innate, but rather only understood as feminine through regular repetitions and cultural citations of what is considered 'normal' for 'feminine'. As Butler writes: 'Gender is performative insofar as it is the *effect* of a regulatory regime of gender differences in which genders are divided and hierarchized *under constraint*' (emphasis in original).[4]

In other words, gender falls under the idea of being performed because gender's performance is repeated over and over again to us. What is considered 'manly' behaviour is only 'manly' because we are shown it over and over again, with the idea that culture points to it and reads it as 'manly'. The constraint Butler describes is the cultural construction of what is 'normal', and our ability to take this all in and then reiterate within our own performances is the effect.

As we grow up, we are taught what is considered 'girl' behaviour and what is not, what is considered 'boy' behaviour and what is not. We have gendered toys – girls play with dolls while boys play with trucks. In school uniforms, girls are given skirts while boys are given trousers. These are examples of how we begin gendering very early, constructing identities of girlhood and boyhood from a young age to demonstrate the continually presented 'girl' which reflects what the society deems as 'girl'. This is important, because not all societies see 'girl' or 'boy' in the same way. Some cultures have very different understandings and definitions of what each gender means, because their performances are different in their different contexts. On top of that, not all cultures have binary genders: many around the world have three, or even more, genders, each with their own performance, definition and understanding.

When cosplayers think about whether or not the cosplay they are going to do is a drag cosplay or a gender-bend, or whether it fits their own conceptions of how they feel about their body, they are engaging with these performances of gender. If the outfit Bailey slaved over for months is suddenly too fem, it is because Bailey is seeing the reflections of what fem means and feeling their body does not suddenly feel comfortable in that social definition of feminine.

In fact, non-binary cosplayers are perhaps more aware of these distinctions of gendered life than other participants are. Sociological research demonstrates most non-binary people have a heightened awareness of the subtle ways social life is binarily gendered. In order to live outside of the binary, they became experts in it.[5] This means they come to understand the subtleties of hair style, clothing and bodily performance in order to emphasize or play down certain aspects to try and carve out an understanding of what a non-binary gendered performance looks like to them.

Drag cosplaying can have serious consequences for some people. For many, the choice to do specific drag cosplays comes with safety issues. While at cons, I encountered many female-identifying people cosplaying male characters, as well as non-binary people cosplaying binary genders. There were far fewer male cosplayers in female-coded costumes. Male cosplayers – or even cosplayers who are read by viewers as male regardless of their actual gender – wearing feminine costumes risk harassment, both verbal and physical. One cosplayer told me that often transphobia, particularly fear of the transwoman, and homophobia are inherently present in these threats.

The performance of gendered identity is also demonstrated in how cosplayers do gender-bending cosplays. Here cosplayers take a character who is canonically identified as one gender and then play them as a different gender, typically the cosplayer's own. This can be understood in a variety of ways. Some actively alter costumes to fit the typical performance of a particular gender in order to have it more clearly read as the gender they want to convey. For others, gender-bending can be more subtle, and more implicitly understood as such by the cosplayer themself rather than the audience. We saw this type of gender-bending in Holly's discussion about their non-binary body having the effect that all their costumes are inherently non-binary. Either way, gender-bending is a way of cosplaying which puts the individual in direct negotiation between the piece of media they choose and their own body.

Elliot, for example, talked about how they typically only gender-bend because of their own body. They talked about how, at first, they would simply cosplay the character as it was faithfully without thinking about gender. However, soon they had to reconsider. 'I used to be a lot about the perfectionism,' they said. 'I used to be like, no, they're male. I have to, I have to pretend I'm a guy now. But, when I started working on Jotaro, I was like, "I'm never ever gonna get in a binder and make it look like him." So I just kind of, I just went, let's embrace it. I'll be a woman.'

Other cosplays shift the character because they want to see a particular representation. One female-identifying cosplayer told me they typically gender-bend male characters because they disliked how female characters are written, a complaint echoed frequently in my interviews. Instead of searching to find a female character they saw a connection to, they made a male character female. 'It doesn't change the story at all, really,' they said with a shrug.

Most gender-bending is from male character to female performance, though sometimes people cosplay female characters as male. Arthur told me about how they considered doing this, because they felt most comfortable cosplaying male characters but sometimes felt an affinity to female characters. Gender-bending them would solve the problem of how to cosplay them.

Many cosplayers expressed the underlying fear and risk involved in male and masculine-facing cosplayers appearing in feminine dress. For them, gender-bending allowed these more masculine cosplayers to cosplay female characters without fear for their own safety.

Many cosplayers told me their performance of character did not change, whether they were doing a drag cosplay or they were gender-bending. The gender of the character was less important than other aspects of the character's movements, thoughts and actions in the world as expressed by the cosplayer. For example, Riley commented on a gender-swapped Jack Skellington from *Nightmare Before Christmas* they did for a photoshoot. When posing, they weren't thinking, 'Oh, well, now he's a woman', but rather focusing on the non-gendered aspects of the form: the shape and silhouette. 'It was just like, this is this silhouette. Now it has a curve to it, has structure to it, I now have very long white hair. That was that.' Riley continued to reflect on their gender-bent characters, stating there was no forward planning. 'As the planning goes along, it just either will stay its gender or I will try to change its gender. I don't think I actively think "I'm gonna make this this."'

Despite how popular gender-bending is, it's not without its critics. Adrian reflected on how they typically dislike gender-bending because of how simplistic it appears. 'Some – for example – are people like "this is my girl version as blank character." And, like, it's just the same but they'd have long hair and a skirt on. It feels like, kind of, not to really be active. You know what I mean? Like it just feels kind of like: skirt on, it's woman now. You know?'

Adrian's critique echoes the way people understand the social conception of gender. For most social plays of 'female', a skirt is present where it's not present in representations of 'male'. While these dynamics are beginning to be questioned in fashion, it's still a strong representation of the way gender dynamics are played and performed by society.

In the examples given of drag cosplay or gender-bending cosplay, the focus is primarily on the gendered performance of the character. However, cosplay can change more than just the character's gender. In several cases, it has actually led to changes in the cosplayer's own understanding of gender. As Arthur told me, and was reflected in the experience of others, cosplay provided a more-or-less safe space for people to play with gender and gender representation. By allowing individuals to temporarily embody a gender performance, cosplayers were able to more readily understand their own gender.

Mason, for example, talked about how cosplay gave them a safe space to think about their own gender, which eventually led to their transition. 'I've always struggled with my gender identity,' they told me.

> I was playing *Overwatch* and I realized there was a guy called Hanzo. And he has my haircut and it's a top knot. And I was like, nine or ten. And I was like, 'Mom, I need to have a top knot like this character in this game because he looks so cool. And I want to look like him.' And then I started getting into cosplay. And I was like, slowly realizing that I didn't want to just dress up as a guy, I was a guy . . . it really helped me realize who I was a lot quicker than it probably would have if I didn't start cosplaying.

Mason is not the only person I spoke to who benefited from cosplay's freedom with gender expression. Arthur, for example, also found cosplay one of the many helpful activities that allowed them to better understand their gender: 'Through cosplay, I'm able to explore that and explore femininity and masculinity and enjoy unity.'

This is not to say that all cosplayers who wear characters of a different gender are bound to transition. Stevie, for example, is a cis cosplayer who often wears costumes of another gender in drag cosplays. For them, it feels more comfortable, fits better with the people they choose to cosplay with and also gives them a sense of security while at conventions.

Connected to gender is cosplay and sexuality. Of particular interest is the popularity of 'sexy' cosplays, when cosplayers take a character and make the costume purposefully risqué. Most cosplayers partaking in sexy cosplays are female identifying and become very visibly present on social media. Due to their popularity on social media, sexy cosplays have also promoted the idea of cosplay more generally as something to be sexualized. Several porn sites have a 'cosplay' tag for people to search. One cosplayer told me they were interviewed about cosplay and immediately asked 'Is it a sex thing?' The sexualized aspect of cosplay has become so widespread that it has begun to take over outside perceptions of cosplay and its purpose.

'I think sometimes when you tell people, "Oh, I cosplay", that's the immediate thing they go to,' Riley told me. 'They expect when you show them a picture of your cosplay, they're gonna see you in a bikini version of whatever this character is. And then they're like, "Oh, this is you dressed as a man."'

Riley's description demonstrates how sexualized cosplay has come to define cosplay for many people. Once on the inside of the community, there is definitely some of that, but it is not the majority. While some cosplayers bemoaned to me how sexy cosplays are a new phenomenon brought on by social media and the rise of Only Fans, others argued against this, including Bailey: 'This is about people not knowing their history,' they told me, visibly annoyed. 'They're like "cosplay was wholesome," and I'm like, have you seen any photographic evidence of worldcons from the '60s and '70s? It was all people with no clothes on in frog masks. There it was – they were all just naked!'

During my interviews, the conversation around sexy cosplays was highly controversial. Some celebrated cosplayers doing sexy versions, while others were angry at them for popularizing the idea of cosplay as sexual. One commented to me that they didn't understand it at all and wished people would just stop.

People who do sexy cosplays had a lot of different reasons, and not all of them were female. Cosplayers of all genders engage in them. The most cited reason was a growth in confidence. Avery, a sexy cosplayer I spoke to, was surprisingly quiet and shy, though they expressed how confident they feel once they're in costume. In fact, they said their favourite thing about cosplay is 'being able to wear whatever you want and feel comfortable'. For some, creating sexually suggestive versions was their way of putting their own spin on the character and making their mark on the media form. While some people change the costume to make it more comfortable or change the hair to fit their ethnic background, these cosplayers change it to fit a particular aesthetic.

The conception of cosplay as sexual does have a negative effect on the community. Convention attendance comes with safety concerns for many cosplayers. Despite many cons proclaiming 'cosplay is not consent', they still raise the issue of people making or suggesting sexual advances or touching without asking. Elliot told me of their hesitation to do what they called 'risky' characters. 'I just don't want creepy people around,' they said. 'I just don't want anything bad to happen, to be honest.'

Some people blamed the sexy cosplayers for these uncomfortable and terrifying positions they were put in. However, those who did sexy cosplays complained that just because they wore more

Sexy cosplayer Aiden (@stormstruckcosplay) at MCM London 2023.

revealing costumes did not mean they necessarily welcomed such experiences either. As the saying 'cosplay is not consent' implies, just because someone wears a revealing outfit doesn't mean they welcome sexual advances.

Avery, who frequently wears suggestive costumes, openly told me of their uncomfortable moments of inappropriate interactions with audience members. Some would touch him while getting photos. The most alarming story was one where they were walking through a very crowded con, with movement limited. While pushing through, someone grabbed Avery's genitals. They were so scared and affected by the sexual assault that they left early and took a long time to recover. Even though Avery wears sexy cosplays, this does not mean they approve or condone the inappropriate behaviour from individuals that other cosplayers fear. Blaming sexy cosplayers for these instances just repeats the misogynistic blame often put on rape victims based on what they're wearing. What the cosplayer is wearing should not allow any level of sexual assault.

Sam refused to call them sexy cosplays and instead referred to them as 'lewd'. 'That one has struck a nerve once or twice here,' they said, 'where I see someone has taken like a brassière and a mini skirt and a wig and been like "professional cosplay".' They pitched their voice higher when saying 'professional cosplay' to sound more feminine. 'Where I see other people pouring their hearts and souls into it, that's probably the only thing that actually irks me a little.'

In contrast, Bailey defended those who wear a bra, mini skirt and wig and call it cosplay. 'They're good cosplayers,' they insisted. 'But it's when they're like, oh, I've glued some things to a bikini? Absolutely valid. Absolutely valid to cosplay.' They reflected that what makes a good cosplay is simply having fun. 'There's nothing wrong with what she's doing. If it makes her happy, whatever, don't care.'

When discussing how several professional cosplayers who tend to do sexy cosplays also have an Only Fans account on the side, or some other way of monetizing their outfits, Bailey continued to be dismissive of any criticism. 'Why would it bother me that somebody else is getting paid to do that far more successfully than Instagram?' they asked with a shrug. 'It's like – you know what – if there's an audience for it, and if you're comfortable doing it, and if it makes you happy and pays your bills, why not?'

When first asked about sexy cosplayers, Arthur gave a sigh. 'People have a lot of hatred for sex workers in general and that comes across in the cosplay community as well,' they said. They discussed having friends who did sexy cosplay, and how others in the community dismissed them or treated them poorly for their costumes.

Another cosplayer discussed that it's hard to cosplay any female costume without it being seen as, in some way, bordering on sexy cosplay. When reflecting on the characters they enjoyed from Japanese anime, they all had very short skirts and crop tops or low-cut shirts. 'How am I supposed to cosplay that properly without being sexy?' they complained.

Some had more nuanced approaches to sexy cosplayers. Mason, for example, commented that they do not believe sexy cosplayers should be allowed at cons, though they have no problem with them existing more generally:

So I feel like I don't have a problem with the sexy cosplayers doing like Only Fans, but I do feel very strongly about when they come to a convention . . . I was at a con and there was a girl in a Playboy bunny latex costume with three kids next to her – like young six-year-olds. And obviously, it's – you come to the con, you expect that. But I feel like if I was bringing my kids, I'd be like, 'Oh, wow, I didn't expect to see that today.'

Some thought sexy cosplays are simply one aspect of what cosplay is and should not be restricted. Stevie, for example, stated that cosplay 'is artistic, and so can take any form'. Others would also see barring certain types of cosplay at cons as problematic. If characters can be naturally more sexualized, then what denotes the difference between sexy cosplays and cosplays of sexualized characters? If one is allowed in certain spheres and the other isn't, the difference between them needs to be clearer.

Stevie addressed the issue of figuring out the difference between the aim of the cosplayer and the natural costume the cosplayer is embodying. Stevie told me about friends of theirs who had posted photos in a costume and received responses assuming that the cosplayer was aiming to be seen as sexy. There was a difference of intent, they stressed to me.

In fact, several cosplayers, including Stevie, voiced their dislike of the over-sexualization of female characters, which led them to frequently choose to cosplay male characters. Blake told me about a new cosplay they had worked on of a female character. After posting a photo online, they were so surprised by the sexualized comments that they were immediately uncomfortable wearing it again. Several cosplayers told me how they were approached by the public differently when wearing more feminine cosplays versus more masculine ones, regardless of the cosplayer's own gender. Part of the problem is what both Bailey and Arthur discussed in relation to sexy cosplays. Whenever I asked about sexy cosplays to my participants, most of the conversation was automatically related to professional cosplayers who post online and also have variations available on separate sites for payment. Very well-known cosplayers, such as Jessica Nigri, are popular examples. In fact, Jessica was name-checked by Sam in their complaint about sexy cosplays. More sexual versions of characters are often immediately associated with professional cosplayers. The response by Arthur immediately fell to that, when they commented on there being nothing wrong with it if it's something you're comfortable doing and it 'pays the bills'.

What was also interesting in these conversations was the immediate assumption of pronouns to associate with these cosplayers. Most of them automatically referred to sexy cosplayers with female pronouns, which makes the assumption that only women partake in this type of cosplay. It allows male cosplays that are often shirtless not to fall into this category, while female characters – whose original forms are already sexualized – immediately fall into a separate category. I attended many conventions in which male cosplayers wore shirtless costumes, such as Kratos from *God of War*, which didn't seem to get as much of the attention in my conversations as women.

Despite the outward appearance of cosplay as being primarily for women, it is a hobby enjoyed by all genders. The interesting aspect of cosplay in relation to gender is its ability to give people a safe space to play with gender and gender socialized experience. This means cosplayers are given a unique opportunity to see gender as fluid and performative. Cosplay therefore allows them to see the world differently and, in return, see themselves differently.

Sexy cosplays are only a small part of the more complicated world of cosplay. That being said, they do exist, and are heavily contested in the community. From the perspective of sexy cosplayers themselves, they see their type of cosplay as equal and just as valid as all the other existing forms. Others see it as a complicated element which leads to dangerous interactions.

Personally, I see sexy cosplay as a transformative element to the cosplay, as transformative as changing the costume or the character's gender. It is part of how the narrative is understood and interpreted by the cosplayer. It is their stamp on the media, their version that makes the character and the media their own. This does not remove the danger and risk that some people face at cons. However, it is important to put the blame for this on the perpetrators who believe their actions are sanctioned, rather than on cosplayers.

8

The Transformative Art
of Cosplay

At the beginning of this book, we sketched out how popular culture is our contemporary mythology. The way we have seen individuals interact with fiction has provided insights into how meaningful popular culture can be for many cosplayers. But one of the great powers of cosplay is its ability to transform both the individual and fiction in its representation. Black cosplayers making characters their own to feel more comfortable in the fictional body, gender-bending characters to fit what the cosplayer wants to portray and even sexy cosplays can all transform the original character in a way which best reflects the cosplayer.

Mythic transformation is not exactly new. Many versions of myths exist, with alterations which pop up in different times and from different storytellers. For many, the assumption is that alterations to the oral record are simply due to the fact that it is not written down. Oral recitation is seen as less reliable than writing, and therefore changes are due to inept storytellers. However, oral recitation has actually been shown to be incredibly reliable.

So what's happening in mythic transformation? For this, we can turn to anthropologist Seth Kunin. Kunin discussed the open transformational power of myth and how myth – as well as ritual – could be transformed to fit the context of the storyteller and community. Kunin referred to this as 'jonglerie' – the juggling of multiple identities and conceptions.[1] For example, a storyteller may struggle to balance their identity as a woman while in a story of deep misogyny, or they may be balancing multiple ethnic or nationalistic identities which may be in conflict at times. Kunin demonstrates how individuals will actively change aspects of narratives to fit their own times.

This is because transformations to a story are necessary for its survival. Times change, needs change and what the community looks for in a myth can alter. If a myth is a narrative that a community uses to understand themselves and the world around them, then when their worldview shifts, so, too, do their myths. In Chapter One, I described my connection to *The Lord of the Rings* and how I found comfort in its frank depiction of post-traumatic stress. This was because my personal experiences caused a radical shift in my worldview, which meant I needed to seek out new myths to reflect this shift. Transformations can also work in reverse – an active need to transform your society's worldview can cause you to seek and frequently tell new myths to push the society towards these changes. There can also be other kinds of transformations such as new interpretations, settings or perspectives on a familiar myth. New audiences can insert people like them into a story that previously omitted them.

Fandom often takes advantage of these transformations, and actively takes control of them. This is because narratives are not set in stone. Even where narratives are written rather than oral, transformations still happen. As Kunin has shown us, we actively need and want to alter narratives to fit our environment.

Michel de Certeau described readers as 'poachers' in someone else's environment, and scholar Henry Jenkins uses this idea of 'poachers' to extend to fanfiction and fandom more generally.[2] Fans are people who are active participants, not passive consumers. As active participants, they will seldom leave things alone and untouched.

One way fans demonstrate their poacher identities is in the nature of head-canon. If the canon is what is considered 'canonical' and present in the original media, head-canon is what individual fans wish was present in the original material and read into it. Head-canons can involve ways of understanding individual characters, romantic relationships the fans wish to see or new interpretations on events. Through their various engagements with the text, whether it be fanfiction, cosplay, video essays or in other ways, fans can express their head-canon not only to fulfil their own desire to see it lived out in some form, but to share it with others. This extends the head-canon beyond one person's head to the community's head.

Cosplay has seemingly always been a part of the fandom scene. Lingering from the 1930s and potentially even earlier, cosplay has been an important facet of the fandom experience, alongside other types of creative fandom, such as fanfiction. Academic studies of fandom have tended to focus on more text-based facets like fanfiction. In some ways, cosplay is like fanfiction. It allows fans to take control of narratives and transform them to their own purposes.

Play is important here – it's serious, sure, but it's also incredibly playful. Fans initiate this play by first engaging with the piece of popular culture with belief. We initially think of engaging with popular culture as a suspension of *dis*belief, but this isn't exactly how things work either. We don't go into a movie or a video game or a book looking for a way in to believe; rather we get taken out of it instead. Basically, it's not a suspension of disbelief, but rather a willingness to believe.

What this comes down to is the way individuals, and fandom in particular, play with notions of belief and involvement in the texts. We tend to think of belief as steadfast and solid. Saying 'I believe' is firm and immovable. But that's not really how belief works. Belief is malleable, and people can play within the boundaries and elements of belief. Belief is, in essence, performed.[3]

As noted in Chapter Three, Richard Schechner, a scholar in the study of performance, proposed two types of play: 'make believe' and 'make belief'. The first maintains the set boundaries between what is considered real and what is considered pretend. The second, however, intentionally blurs them.[4] Schechner, therefore, questions how much a performer believes their own performance in order to distinguish between the two. Jane McGonigal argues against this and sees it as problematic to rely purely on a performer's self-awareness of their belief and performance, because this can change and fluctuate. Instead, McGonigal posits different questions to distinguish them, particularly the pleasures and pay-offs of feigned belief in a play, or how the practices of performed belief can influence performers in their daily life post-performance.[5]

Perhaps most similar to this particular view of belief performance is Michael Kinsella, who did some work on legend-tripping, which is when people take a journey to a specific location or perform an action which, according to legend, has the potential to trigger supernatural experiences.[6] Legend-tripping relies on the idea of 'ostensive acts', or the ways in which 'real'-life activities are guided by legends or mythology.[7] Legend-tripping uses ostensive acts in order to trigger such experiences, so the two work in tandem, and both work to blur the traditional binary of 'reality' and 'fiction'. Kinsella comments that legend-trippers perform the strange intermingling between fantasy and reality with the purpose more towards exploitation of emotion in performance, rather than in proving some objective existence of the supernatural.

Both Kinsella and McGonigal help to explore a new avenue of how we can understand belief in a post-Enlightenment Western world. Rather than an individual's sense of 'in' or 'out' when it comes to belief, we should instead think of belief as a scale of possibilities.

I like to think of belief as a community pool.[8] There is a deep end, in which some may completely immerse themselves in the waters of belief, diving in head first. But there is also an incline into a shallow end, where some may prefer to stand in the waist-height waters of belief. Others may drift from side to side, paddling from one end to the other, but never wanting to get their hair wet. Some may dip their feet in the pool, gently spinning their toes in belief. And even others are still there, speaking to those in the waters but staying outside the pool – electing instead to sit on a beach chair and read a book. Yet, we would still describe all of them as being 'at the pool'.

The analogy of the pool and its waters of belief allow us to understand how belief is rarely firm and set. Individuals in a particular religion – where belief is typically considered far stronger – may still not be married to any particular belief typically ascribed to their religion. In fact, individuals may shift where they emphasize the intensity of their religion, sometimes in beliefs, sometimes not, and sometimes in different beliefs than before.

I first encountered this type of malleability of belief when doing research with Christian Scientists in Edinburgh. On paper, Christian Scientists 'believe' Western medication is not effective and not real. While sitting in on a Wednesday evening meeting, I witnessed one of the women, one who had been particularly vocal about the importance of Christian Science teaching, take an ibuprofen. Even though taking this medication is technically against the beliefs of Christian Science, she rationalized the action to me through a rounded discussion of how she understands that medication does not affect her as much as prayer, but that it 'helps'.

Belief is malleable, constantly shifting in nature and, in Kinsella's terms, able to be manipulated. It is inherently something which can be performed and played with. This playing with belief is what allows cosplayers to actively make fundamental changes to the original piece of media so effectively.

A fan of *The Lord of the Rings*, for example, can temporarily believe in its world when watching the movies, as we tend to do, and afterwards believe in the core of what it's saying. These are two different types of belief. Cosplayers then allow other people who love the world to dive back temporarily into the waters when they see the characters walking around and interacting with them. This means that when cosplayers make alterations to the characters and transform them in some way, this is a fundamental transformation in the original media.

The thing about mythology, folklore and stories more generally is they can always be subversive. Sometimes this is in very obvious and loud ways. More often, though, it's quieter and more hidden, but always there, working away in the shadows. This is because stories are always from people – so much so that I believe people *are* stories. We are defined by them, explained by them, connect through them. Every conversation I have with a friend is a form of a story. Every cherished memory I share with my husband is a story I hold close to my heart. To be human is to tell stories. And because we are social beings, and the stories we tell are also an intricate part of our social and cultural landscapes, the stories we tell are also social beings. As social beings themselves, they are just as influenced by our ideological foundations as everything else that is 'us'.

The downside of this is that our stories can cement social narratives of oppression. Patriarchy and racism can become embedded in the narratives that are embedded in the culture. Just as misogyny and transphobia can appear in our culture, they can also appear in our stories. Unfortunately, when this happens, it can cement these aspects of our society.

But stories can also change. We can actively transform our narratives and alter aspects of them. We can actively alter our narratives to fit the new contexts we find ourselves in. We can change narratives from racist to anti-racist, from transphobic to trans inclusive. People do not have to adhere to oppressive social systems – they can also reject them. And when we reject certain power structures, we begin to see which narratives continue these structures and which do not. We can change the narratives which reaffirm structures of oppression and alter them to shift the narratives to fit a different ideology. And through these alterations of narrative, we can try and change our society itself.

For Kinsella, in his definition of legend and legend-telling, they are inherently able to be subversive. Legends are 'context-dependent' and inherently 'performative'. They are able to identify and channel all the anxieties and ideologies of communities and folk groups.[9]

Cosplay is a type of storytelling, and as such also has the potential to be as subversive as other forms of story. As a form of mythic performance, cosplayers have the ability to transform our myths and narratives and alter them to reflect the ideologies of their own communities. As the cosplayer's own ideologies and anxieties alter, so, too, do their interpretations and the forms the story takes. By transforming the narrative in their performances, cosplayers are able to shift the interpretation of the original work. The criticism or reflection or alteration being levied against the original piece of media is carried forward and impacts individual audience members as well as the performer.

Cosplay begins with a story. It starts the minute a cosplayer watches a movie or television show, plays a video game or reads a book, forming a connection with a character or a piece of media. The connection can occur for a variety of reasons, some of which are incredibly personal, while others are more practical.

One cosplayer commented that they typically gravitate to characters who have characteristics they want to embody. We saw this in Sam, who cosplayed a character who had gone through a similar loss to them but who coped with it in a way they wanted to emulate. Elliot picked characters like them, and told me they know instantly when watching something if the character is one they are going to cosplay. Riley reflected on how the process of understanding their connection to characters is sometimes slow to come to them and is part of a process that becomes more obvious the more work they put into the cosplay itself. Stevie, in contrast, talked about the importance of balancing between a cosplay of a character you like and one you want to wear, noting that sometimes they want to see a character they like but not be them.

Whether it's because of their practical style, such as Mia who preferred the style of female characters who were childlike, or whether it's a personal connection to the character's personality, the cosplay is chosen from a standing narrative. The character fits within this narrative and fills a particular role. The character has a personality and a way of holding themselves which needs to be as present in the performance of the cosplay as the character's outfit.

In one of my conversations, Mia actively complained about when cosplayers don't perform their character 'properly'. Their primary example was a group of people at a con all cosplaying as Sasuke from *Naruto*. They complained about seeing them 'jumping around' and acting 'silly', which they believed did not fit Sasuke's character. The various views and experiences of performance we explored in the second chapter are all about this complicated notion of character action.

Cosplayers are tasked with telling a story through their cosplay, whether they are completely immersed in their performances like Sam, or only really pose for photos like Adrian, or see performance as flexible like Elliot. Regardless of their approach, part of the experience of cosplay is in the story it tells and the way individuals use their cosplay to tell the stories they want in the way they want.

The idea of telling a story nonverbally is not unique or new. Any dancer will tell you the importance of storytelling without words – the way they move their body around air or other bodies is done with the utmost practice and purpose. Each movement is performed to tell the story they have plotted out.

Anthropologist Claude Lévi-Strauss believed that without proper inscriptions, bodies fail to be social persons.[10] We need to have certain things ascribed on to us, in the form of clothes or actions, in order to be social. And the reverse is also true: we can put on certain things in order to appear to represent the social identities we want. Cosplayers put on the inscriptions of other characters in the form of clothing, props and even the way they hold the body, in order to act out that particular social identity.

Stories have always been told in a variety of ways. Even traditional narratives were told with more than just words. Performers (and I use this word as opposed to 'actors' for a reason) may don a mask and dance or move in ways to tell the story of the character.

Cosplay, in more ways than one, is a mask performers wear. They adorn themselves like the character, and like the performers of old mythic tales they must also take their performance seriously and act the part to the best of their ability. Cosplayers, like other performers of narrative, have agency over their story. The story is not told passively through them, but actively. They choose to tell the stories in the way they feel most compelled to through the presence of the narrative in their own limbs. And because the story is always given to performers with this level of agency, the story is also capable of being subverted in order to fit meanings or interpretations the performers wish to communicate.

There are many ways cosplayers can be subversive in their performance. The agency creators and performers have over their cosplays also means they leverage some level of agency over the narrative itself. By transforming the narrative in their performances, the shifting interpretation being levied on the original narrative, or the criticism or reflection being asked of the original narrative, is also carried forward and impacts individual audience members, as well as the performer themselves. Most of these social critiques or differing interpretations are concerned with discussions or representations of gender.

In the previous chapter, we explored the dynamics of gender and gender alterations that happen frequently in cosplay. We discussed how gender itself is a typical social performance. Judith Butler uses the word 'performativity' to describe how gender is performed. When discussing subversion, we can see that these performative acts of gender can also be called a social myth of gender – a story of what it means to be a particular gender which is told and retold by society. If our performance of the myth of gender changes, it can alter our understanding of the gender.

In other words, society has already taught us what it is to perform 'female' and presents us with what is essentially the 'myth of female' – a story of what it means to be a woman or feminine. By putting on female when the performer isn't actually female, we see gender as a performance rather than something inherent. In fact, Judith Butler's work on 'performativity' often related back to drag performances, where the performance of gender is displayed as an overt performance.

When cosplayers perform a gender-bending cosplay, they are relying not just on the performance of their character, but on the performance of gender. Even though a defining characteristic of the original character – their gender – has been altered, the audience needs to still understand the performance is of the original character. But combined with that, the cosplayer also has to perform gender. They have to tell the story of the chosen gender.

As Adrian said, gender-bending cosplays cannot be simple. Adrian stated they disliked it when cosplayers put on 'long hair and a skirt' to make it a female version. What Adrian was picking up on is that a gender-bend is more complicated. Riley commented that the decision to make a character into a gender-bend comes from the costuming process rather than any kind of self-consideration. They talked about making a female version of Jack Skellington from *Nightmare Before Christmas* but deciding to keep Lucious from *Our Flag Means Death* as male; in both cases, it was because of how making the costumes panned out rather than because they desperately wanted to alter the gender.

Gender-bend cosplays subvert audience expectations on two fronts. The first is the expectation of the original character. By presenting the original character as true to form with only the simple alteration of gender, it subverts our social understanding of gender as a hierarchical definition of self. The performative narratives surrounding gender help to solidify typical social norms which work by suppressing and oppressing gender binaries and differences. By breaking these, cosplayers are able to demonstrate that gendered performance is more innate and does little to alter the cosplay itself.

Performing with just gendered differences demonstrates how little they can affect a character. A character's strength or importance can remain unchanged even with the shift of gender. This is where the second subversion in gender-bend can occur. Any performance of a character is going to come accompanied by the performance of the gender itself. For gender-bending, that performance is in the presentation of the character's altered gender – performing the original character as inherently 'girl' or 'boy'. Like drag, this performance causes the audience to consider gender's social performance and its malleability.

We should, however, consider that not all forms of subversion purposefully work to break social norms. This is referred to as a type of 'anti-structure' by anthropologist Victor Turner.[11] Turner looked at how many rituals seem to break the confines of our social worlds. People act differently from their ascribed normality during rituals, sometimes purposefully acting out different roles entirely. While this initially appears to be socially subversive, Turner points out how this moment of 'anti-structure' actually allows individuals to go back to their strict social norms more comfortably, thereby helping to maintain the social structure rather than break it. Judith Butler also saw this in drag performances. Not all drag performances are the same, but Butler noted how some which performed gender in a particularly direct way actually worked to uphold the social hierarchies and definitions of the various genders rather than to break them.[12]

But that's not to say all forms of gender-bending cosplay or drag cosplay are necessarily supporting rather than subverting the social structure. Nor is the play with gender the only way that cosplay can work to be subversive, regardless of the type of sub-version. It's a pivotal example of how cosplays can be altered, and how this altering of the character can fundamentally change audience expectations.

Racial alterations happen frequently. One Black cosplayer explained how they frequently change the original character's hair to be more akin to Black hair. In this way, they are able to see themselves more in the art form they are performing and show a bit of themselves and their background in their performance of char-acter. Again, the alteration helps to demonstrate the importance of Black representation and the performance of Black identities. By bringing this into the sphere of popular culture, where Black char-acters are often rare to find, they are able to subvert the concept of what it means to be a part of fandoms and what kind of fandoms these cosplayers wish to have. Typically, fans of pop culture media like Japanese anime or video games are thought of as white. The presence of Black cosplayers helps to alter this narrative and brings attention to the fact that many people can be fans.

The alteration of characters simply by having Black skin also demonstrates the lack of representation often found in media. It shows overtly that Black bodies exist and have a place in media more generally, and in the cosplay community more specifi-cally. That being said, Black cosplayers are often faced with racist backlash both online and at cons from people who reject the social alterations happening whenever a Black cosplayer wears a costume.

Other cosplayers also face adversity simply through their existence. Muslim women often use their hijabs and other head coverings as part of their cosplay. Some style their hijabs like wigs, while others take creative liberties to understand how the character would wear a hijab, in a similar way to Black hairstyles. This has also sparked a backlash. One cosplayer who often wore Captain America cosplays in their hijab explained how they got comments saying that people like them were not allowed to represent America in this way. By continuing to cosplay, and being visible, hijab-wearing cosplayers actively alter both the conception of the original media and of fandom more widely.

Cosplayers who change the characters to fit their racial or cultural bodies do not necessarily do so with the intention of changing the wider cultural worlds surrounding them. Rather, the transformations they make are for their own comfort and to reflect their own identities. By embracing the aspects of themselves they do not wish to alter, such as their hijab, they are engaging in the negotiation of identities present in cosplay. Cosplays are therefore a joint experience of the relationship between the cosplayer and the text, which has a ripple effect on the wider community.

Transformations of text can also be with the media itself more generally. Cosplayers like to alter the character in creative ways. This can be for physical comfort, personal identity negotiation or simply through creativity. For the last – transformations for creativity's sake – sometimes cosplayers take liberties with characters by transforming their origins. These 'alternative universe' cosplayers change recognizable characters by imagining them in a different genre. A popular version of alternative universe cosplays I saw was a steampunk version of Sherlock Holmes. In fact, steampunk was a popular choice for cosplayers to use to alter narratives.

As we have seen throughout many of our examples and through the previous chapters, cosplay is more than just exact reproduction. While some do seek out ideal replication of character, not every cosplayer does. Transformations in costume or character can be for a multitude of reasons. These personal choices have a direct effect on the community surrounding the cosplayer. This is not always necessarily just positive or negative. Black cosplayers, for example, create active change in the community by being more visible, but face a lot of negative feedback from people who resist change.

These choices of transformation, whether genre, race, culture or gender, can demonstrate cosplay's ability to be subversive. Cosplayers are active storytellers of the narratives they find a connection to and their performance of these characters, altered the way they choose, can actively change the way wider society thinks or feels about the narratives they are performing. Ultimately, all of these changes are linked to identity, and the way the story interacts with, emphasizes or engages with the cosplayer's sense of self.

9

Storytelling with
Body and Identity

A cosplay performance is displayed on and communicated through the body. The cosplayer's chosen character has to be read in the way the cosplayer poses for photos, moves through a con and is dressed. In the previous chapter, we looked briefly at the way the body moves to tell stories and the way clothing can be used as a form of storytelling performance. Helpful concepts like implicit mythology, discussed in Chapter Three, offered a guide to explain the way stories impact us and the way we think about and move through stories as we tell them and embody them. I think it may be useful now to think more seriously about the bodies of cosplayers, and the way these bodies tell stories and communicate identities.

Our bodies are a fundamental part of us and we can't really talk about communities or cultures or even stories without first thinking about our bodies. Everything that happens to us involves the body in some way. It's through the body that we have our senses, perceptions and experiences; even emotional interactions have bodily reactions, like a racing heart or butterflies in the stomach. We often experience the world differently from others because of our different bodies – the colour of our skin, our perceived gender and our ability to move can all impact the way others interact with us, and therefore impact our understanding of society.

Anthropologist Mary Douglas talked about how each of us carries around two bodies: a physical body and a social body.[1] Our physical body is our biological self, the objective presence of matter in space that we move. But this physical body impacts a more socialized body; we move differently in different spaces because of our perceived social differences, or we are dressed in particular ways to understand those circumstances. Our physical body, like the colour of our skin, can dictate our social standing and the way our social body is understand by others. Similarly, our social body can constrain and dictate what happens with our physical body. People may refrain from body modifications like tattoos or piercings because of a perceived social difference these bodies have, for example. Judith Butler's concept of the performative nature of gender also plays into this – the way our social body performs gender based on the perceived idea of what our physical body may or may not look like.[2]

The way we dress is a part of this. The way I dress when sitting at home playing video games is not the same way I dress when lecturing a room full of undergraduates. This is because my social body is different in each of these situations, and this impacts the way I dress and hold my physical body. At home, I have certain roles I must fulfil, but these are relaxed and domicile roles: I am a wife, and I care for a home. I may be able to wear comfortable sweatpants (which may not have been what I wore hanging around the house when trying to woo my partner), but I still have to be dressed enough to open the door if a parcel arrives or if my partner brings a colleague home after work. Similarly, when I am lecturing in front of a classroom, my social role is no longer related to my partner, but rather to my classroom. I am authoritative and knowledgeable. I may still wear comfortable clothes, but they won't be sweatpants. I may dress more modestly when in front of my classroom than I would out on a date with my partner, because I want to refrain from inappropriate interactions with students. These social interactions dictate the way I dress, the way I speak and the way I hold my body. My husband once commented on how he heard my voice change slightly when I was lecturing compared to the way I speak at home. This is not to say that when I lecture I am pretending – rather the physical body is held to a different social standard and therefore I make certain alterations. In essence, the naked physical body is never actually naked, but constantly clothed in our social and cultural influences.

This is important for a conversation about cosplay because even the fun-loving dressing as fictional characters can't escape these social influences on the body. And often, our understandings of how this dress play happens is also based on considerations of social bodies and their constraints and impact on the physical body. The way we tell stories and the way we interpret and receive these stories are all bodily, and therefore we need to talk about the body and cosplay.

We previously looked at the masquerade, where cosplayers perform a skit or show off their costume in a series of poses on a stage in front of hundreds of people. Sometimes, this is to musical or vocal tracks, but masquerades are always about two things: the costume and the story. While in our previous discussion of masquerades we focused on the skill involved, such as construction and character knowledge, there's another important consideration: the importance of story performance through the body of the cosplayer.

A masquerade performance has three potential avenues: (1) a simple series of poses; (2) a dance or movement routine to music; or (3) a full skit. At one convention, two cosplayers who entered the masquerade together performed a series of scenes from their chosen television show, with the original voice actors of the show played out on loudspeakers while the cosplayers lip-synced and acted out the story. Something similar happened to the winner of the masquerade at another convention – a cosplayer combined a series of poses in a scene as they lip-synced to a monologue by the chosen character. In both examples, the cosplayer carefully chose music, dialogue or a scene which best captured the essence of the character they chose to portray.

The cosplayers' bodies must blend somewhere between the social body of themselves as a person and the social body of their character. In both, their physical body is being controlled by their social bodies. A good performance of a character is not necessarily dependent on the look of the physical body, but rather on the way the physical body is moved, dressed and performed.

During my time with cosplayers, I heard over and over again the refrain that you can cosplay anyone you want, regardless of the cosplayer's gender, race, body size or sexual orientation. This all assumes people do not partake in harmful practices such as black-facing. Some white cosplayers did black up their skin in order to portray characters who are darker skinned. While not wide-spread, it was a practice that several of my participants and I have seen at conventions. That being said, I have also seen white cosplayers portraying Black characters without darkening their skin, and through the process of dress, pose and movement were able to communicate their character effectively in a non-harmful way.

Likewise, Black cosplayers are not restricted to choosing only Black characters to portray. Some actively choose to change certain elements of their characters to fit a more Afro-style, as discussed earlier. One cosplayer, for example, told me about how they often choose wigs that are more reminiscent of Black hair, regardless of the original character's hair. Despite the changes to the original character, they are still able to communicate effectively the original character and their relationship to the story in masquerades, competitions and online photographs. These alterations demonstrate how the cosplayer's original social body never goes away. This cosplayer, for example, knows their skin colour dictates much about their social body. They actively decided to blur the boundaries between the two social bodies of themselves and their character, because their social body as the cosplayer inevitably impacts the way they are able to communicate with the physical body.

Fashion, and the way one is dressed, is an important facet of communication and storytelling, and not just for cosplay. Daniel Ben-Amos urged folklorists to look beyond the typical genre-based definitions of folklore and instead look at specific manifestations of folk ideas.[3] In other words, Ben-Amos was asking people to stop focusing on what separates folklore from legend and myth, and instead think about the way people move, speak and act as a demonstration of how we think and act in the world. As we've mentioned before, stories provide an important insight into the way we think about the world around us and the way we fit into it, and these stories can impact us in a variety of ways, including how we live our everyday life. Worldview and stories are intimately intertwined.

We can see this in the way subcultures mark themselves by what they wear. Punk, for example, is both a worldview and an aesthetic focused on communicating its ideals via clothes. We use clothes to communicate our social cohesion, or lack thereof. Our clothing marks us as part of an in-group or our position as the 'Other'.

Our identities, therefore, are inscribed on our body, even in something as innocuous as how we hold it to more detailed body modifications and clothing. Acts of dress play, like cosplay, use these things to perform identity in a variety of ways. Historical re-enactment uses historic research and archaeology to temporarily live the life of historical figures through the performance of ancient identities. Drag is the performance of gender, sometimes for the purpose of playing with stereotypes and social ideas of gender – often performed by someone of a different gender. By moving the body, modifying the body temporarily with foam to change its shape and wearing specific types of clothing, the drag performer is able to perform gender as a type of identity performance. By changing our clothes and the perception of our physical bodies, we can change the way our identities are perceived. Cosplayers get at the heart of this by analysing what makes the characters who they are – what their identities are and how these identities are marked on the body. It's important for them to understand these aspects in order to perform.

Our identities are not set solid somewhere deep within ourselves, but are socially constituted. They are influenced and altered by our social realities, such as the people we hang out with, the rituals we undertake, the narratives we use and surround ourselves with, and the way society treats and interacts with us. We are constantly changing our identities. Most of us are not the same people we were ten or twenty years ago. We've had many experiences, whether big things like traumatic life events or small things like being greatly affected by a movie. We internalize our experiences and they therefore reflect our sense of self. Our parents impact our identity, but so do the interactions we have with our parents as we grow and develop.

We also perform our identity for those around us. Like the gender performance discussed in Chapter Seven and in the previous chapter, parts of our identity are performed for others and *because* of others. Some aspects can be more innately learned, such as gender, but others can be purposeful, like adopting a subcultural style. Tattoos, for example, are a purposefully performed identity that is literally written on our skin.

This means our identities are not fixed but malleable and inherently changeable through our emotions and social performances. The difference between 'girl' and 'not girl' is a social performance, rather than something inherently 'girl'. What makes someone 'Goth' and 'not Goth' is our social performance. Any aspect of in-groups as opposed to out-groups is visible in the way we present ourselves to the social worlds we find ourselves in: from the way we talk to the way we move to the way we dress.

It can also work the other way. When groups interact with us in a way which treats us as the 'Other', we may push back and demonstrate that we are not part of the group. This is called a 'cycle of alterity', or a cyclical spiral of creating and maintaining difference. If someone interacts poorly with a Black cosplayer, marking them as an 'Other', it may further push this cosplayer to demonstrate their difference even more.

This is why acting is a play with identity. By artfully changing the way we dress, move and speak, we can actively change the way the world perceives who we are. As part of a high school initiation into the Drama Club, I had to dress one day as the person who had been actively taking me under their wing. For me, it was a boy a few years older named Chester. As a cis-girl, I took the opportunity to pretend to be another gender as a fun play with identity change. I wore a black wig to hide my long ginger hair. I put on very little make-up and wore baggy clothes. I chose to sit in stereotypically male ways. In fact, I went much further than how Chester would have behaved in the pure joy of my very early drag king impersonation. In one of my classes, a teacher was so surprised by my presence that she almost called to have a strange student removed who wasn't supposed to be there. Even though I didn't look radically different (I hadn't done the extreme elements of professional drag performers such as contouring with make-up, for example), the simple act of changing my mannerisms disrupted the teacher's conception of who I was as a person.

In fact, drag and cosplay have a lot in common in regards to the way they transform identities and play with the alteration as an act of entertaining fun. There are, of course, core differences in the way cosplayers interact and understand their play compared to drag; the primary one I found was the use of pronouns. For drag, the typical way of discussing drag performers is to use the gendered pronoun of their drag persona when referring to that persona, but then to opt for the actor's pronoun when out of drag. For cosplayers, it is typical always to use a cosplayer's pronoun, regardless of their character. This demonstrates a fundamental difference in the way the identity performances are carried out and understood: where drag personas are unique to individuals, cosplays are broadly for the community, meaning there can be many of one specific character at a convention, but at a drag show there is only one of that persona.

Like the difficulty my teacher had recognizing me in drag, I had some trouble recognizing cosplayers out of character. When conducting my research, I often met people at cons or other events where they were in character. When meeting up for a more formal interview or for other types of chatter, they were often out of character and I would struggle to remember who they were. Most of the time it was because their whole demeanour was different. If they were loud and confident in character, they were suddenly demure, shy and withdrawn. Or they had different mannerisms or spoke with a higher pitched voice. These small alterations made it more difficult to recognize the individual in cosplay and out, and that was before also including other alterations such as hair colour and length or make-up.

One thing drag and cosplay, as well as other forms of dress play, show us is the way malleability of identity feeds into performance and play. What makes the performance of characters fun for cosplayers is being a different person for a time. As one of my participants told me repeatedly, 'I just like being someone different.'

If identity is performed, either by characters in fiction or us in our everyday lives, it means this identity can be replicated. Cosplay is often seen as the duplication of characters – viewers sometimes seem to revel in pointing out when cosplays are not as accurate to the original as they could be. While some cosplayers, like Sam for example, enjoy getting things just right and performing consistently in character, others see cosplay as a less exact activity. Another cosplayer I spoke to discussed how they study a costume to decide what they can get away with skipping over when putting it together. They spoke about deciding which aspects of the costume were needed for character recognition. Some elements of the character's aesthetic are important and an easy way for a viewer to immediately recall the character in question. Others actively change outfits or aspects of the full look in order to fit their own cultural and social body, while still maintaining recognizable aspects of the character, as discussed earlier.

These are what sociologist Erving Goffman calls 'identity kits' – parts of a person's aesthetics and bodily appearance which instantly define them as who they are.[4] A friend of mine, for example, always seems to wear a flower print on her body every day. It became a game between me and another friend to see who could spot the flower print in the day. When she found out about it, she was surprised she did that – it was never something she intended when she dressed in the morning. A flower print would, therefore, be part of my friend's identity kit. If I were to try and cosplay her, I would definitely try to include a cute flower print somewhere in my outfit, whether it was the shirt, skirt or even just a simple scarf. On a fictional note, Jim Butcher's character Harry Dresden is often described wearing a long leather trench coat and a silver pentacle. While other aspects of his outfit change – sometimes multiple times in a book – the leather coat and the silver pentacle remain almost constant.

There are other aspects of the person that are more physical. Does the character stand up tall or stoop over as if shy? Are they exuberant and bubbly or quiet and demure? These are also parts of the character's identity that cosplayers pick up on and embody in their performances.

This is not to say that identity is somehow fake. All of our identities are at some level a performance, and these performances are real and have a real presence with a real effect on ourselves and the worlds we inhabit.

Despite similarities between drag and cosplay, there are fundamental differences in the way drag and cosplay approach the play with identity. As mentioned before, the cosplay community insists on the use of the same pronoun for the cosplayer regardless of whether they are in or out of character. Unlike drag, where pronouns are fluid depending on the way the performer is currently dressing, cosplay does not allow for a complete shifting of identity in the same way as drag. In an interview on the Religion and Popular Culture Podcast, cosplayer and writer Holly Swinyard spoke about this aspect of cosplay performance. Holly is non-binary and voiced excitement at being referred to with the proper pronouns and gendered understanding when playing these characters, which doesn't happen in other parts of their life. When asked if they had ever tried to take a character typically gendered male or female and make them non-binary, Holly responded that their body is non-binary, they are non-binary and therefore any character they embody is non-binary the moment it is performed on their body.[5]

This reveals an interesting complication to the way cosplay is performed and understood by cosplayers. For this cosplayer, as well as for many others, cosplay is a joint performance enacted between them and the character being performed. In drag, the character the drag performer is enacting becomes the performer – a complete transformation of self. In contrast, cosplayers often see their performance as a joint experience between the cosplayer and the character – less a complete takeover and more a compromise in which the cosplayer negotiates the amount each identity is recognized by the outside viewer.

Cosplay's negotiation of identities means the performance can affect the character, as Holly mentioned in their embodiment of characters. But the characters can also have an impact on the cosplayer as well. Riley, a mixed-race cosplayer, talked very openly about the constantly shifting racial identities they hold. They spoke to me about sometimes struggling with the idea of which characters they 'should' or 'shouldn't' cosplay, but stressed that, in the end, it doesn't matter:

My relationship with cosplay and my race is that, for me, it just eradicates it. And for some people, it helps them find that and find like relations to them in their race. But for me, it means that I don't have to even think about it. In my day-to-day, not that I struggle with [it], but I'm very conscious of it. And for cosplay, I'm like, it literally doesn't matter. It doesn't matter how I perceive myself and how other people perceive me for just that moment while you're in a cosplay. Doesn't matter.

Riley demonstrates how the act of cosplaying, and the negotiation of identity cosplayers undergo in the construction and performance of the cosplay, can have an effect on the individual. For Riley, the day-to-day experience of being mixed race falls away while in cosplay; they are able to embody whichever character they feel most connected to, and to relax in an act of racial ambiguity.

Emma, likewise, talked about how cosplaying as another person actually means they're being themself. They phrased it as being themself in the form of that character, and how they often reflect on this while they're at cons. The act of being in costume is more than just being another person. Emma, another cosplayer of colour like Riley, reflected on how they struggled at first to find a comfortable middle ground between themself and the characters they wanted to cosplay. Their first cosplay character had a similar skin tone, which they felt comfortable doing because of how rare it is to find anime characters who have non-white skin tones. 'So I just thought, oh, I think I'm only able to, like, cosplay characters in my single skin tone,' they said. 'But then, you know, my friends were like, "No, it doesn't matter your skin tone, just cosplay a character." And I think it helped me a lot to break that barrier as well. I'm like, yeah, I'm going to cosplay. So I'm cosplaying whoever I want to cosplay.' They reflected on how this helped them to see similarities in themself to characters that went beyond skin tone, while still maintaining how important their skin tone was to their sense of self.

Comfort in costumes was repeated frequently in my interviews, but never in the sense that costumes necessarily needed to be comfortable on the skin. Cosplayers often bemoaned how uncomfortable cosplay can be on the body, from the discomfort of tight wigs to clothing that is difficult to move in. Despite this, many participants talked about comfort in cosplay, meaning more a comfort in self. Bailey, for example, reflected on the difference between a bad and a good cosplay being how good you feel wearing it. In the same conversation, they talked about being uncomfortable at a con, but sticking with it because they love how they feel about themself in the outfit and therefore think of it as a good cosplay. Elliot talked about having a 'comfort cosplay' – the cosplay they tend to gravitate to and have the best time in. In each of these instances, cosplayers are regularly performing the character of their cosplay while also acknowledging an alteration in how they understand their own performance of themself.

The experiences of both Riley and Holly demonstrate a fundamental aspect of cosplaying and the cosplay experience: an equal and direct relationship between the cosplayer and the fiction they are inhabiting. This relationship is born from deep engagement with the text in order to formulate the outfit and/or the performance undertaken, and also through the actual act of the performance itself. Holly, for example, talked about how they felt different depending on the character they embodied, discussing how when cosplaying a villain character they felt strange compared to an exuberant over-the-top character – which they said would make them insufferable if they felt that way all the time. In other words, Holly's mood and personal bodily understanding shifted depending on what they were wearing and who they were.

Sam, the excited cosplayer who spun tales of their ability to stay in character and how fun the act of performing has been for them, also had moments of seriousness in our conversation, especially when talking about how certain character choices had a direct impact on their self-understanding and self-expression. When chatting about character choice, for example, Sam mentioned how their choice to play Tohru Honda, one of the primary characters in the anime *Fruits Basket*, was intimately tied to a shared loss:

> I felt so moved to become her, because of all the things she had been through in her life. She had lost her mom, I had lost my mom, like . . . all these things that happen. I was, like, I wish that I could still go out there with a smile on my face at that point in my life. And so I did that, and I did everything I could to be like her when I was in cosplay.

Sam's connection to character was intimately connected to a shared experience of grief. The performance of character, the mask they were able to wear, allowed them – temporarily – to live in a fictional world in which the grief over the loss of their mother did not affect the way they interact in the world. The performance which typically leads to blurring boundaries is always done in fun – this was reiterated by Sam many times, constantly referring to themself as 'enthusiastic' and 'passionate', and talking about how much fun the conventions and cosplays can be – but it also had a very serious effect on Sam. It allowed them to channel feelings of grief and use the fictional worlds they typically only watch to be embodied and therefore to help them cope with loss.

Similarly, Riley discussed their character choices having a deep connection to them: 'So I think on the surface level, I picked a character because I'm like, you look really cool. But if I psychoanalyse myself, even for a second, I'm like, I think these are just characters that I resonate with on some degree, emotionally.'

A lot of the wider conversation about how cosplayers pick their characters is similar to those I had with Sam and Riley. In a documentary, professional cosplayer Jessica Nigri made a similar point, saying she picks characters she really wishes she could emulate, for example.[6] This also echoes Chapter One's discussion of cosplay's connection to mythology and how cosplayers see a deep connection to self in their narratives of choice.

But as my participant Charlie stressed, play underpins everything. Cosplay is the play in costumes – it's not just about the costume, but the play element has to be involved as well. The play does not necessarily mean more serious elements of emotional connection are not important or fully present – with play, things can be serious and real for participants at the same time as being entertaining and playful. Sam does not think they are truly Tohru Honda, for example. They know they are 'Sam' wearing a costume and play-acting, but the act allows them to – even if only temporarily – take on aspects of Tohru they wish they had. For just a moment, Sam was able to live how Tohru does – smiling through grief.

This is all a form of 'as if' play – a playful act of potential. Like wrestler fans and the art of kayfabe, cosplayers enjoy the playful act of cosplaying 'as if' they are truly the characters they embody. The 'as if' play works along the lines of the mask, allowing the performer to temporarily blur the boundaries between the physical and the fictional. The act of cosplay allows individuals to directly impact the fictions they love through their act of embodiment, but they also are impacted back by the fictions. It's a reciprocal relationship.

As much as we see cosplayers changing and altering understandings of characters, cosplayers also are changed and altered themselves through the act of cosplay. This is not to say, of course, that they are somehow the strange fanatic 'Others' some popular media like to portray them as. As much as cosplayers are impacted by the fictions they love and embody, they do not lose sight of which part is fiction and which part is not. Despite the blurring of the two worlds, they know full well what's real and what's not. In fact, that makes it far more interesting – cosplayers know precisely the way fiction impacts them, and they also know precisely how they are changing and altering fiction with their embodiment.

In a way, cosplay is a type of fanfiction, though acted in a completely different way. Fanfiction is one way fans of pop culture directly interact with their objects of fandom. Fanfiction writers take the original pieces of popular culture and alter it in their own image. An overview of the history of fanfiction is far too complicated and frankly unnecessary for our purposes here. What is important for our study of cosplay is how fanfiction narratives stand in contrast and comparison to the original piece of popular culture, such as a television show or novel. There are a lot of comparisons which can be drawn between fanfiction and cosplay. For example, as Henry Jenkins discusses in his work, fanfiction demonstrates that readers are not passive audiences but active 'poachers', using creativity and agency to engage with the narratives which they have a deep emotional connection to.[7] In the case of fanfiction, fans craft their own narratives based on the stories they love, and take them in new and interesting directions. They may, for example, take a narrative and tell it from a different character's perspective or they may add new characters to the same world. In some cases, they take greater agency over the story and change important elements to make a social point. One well-known fanfiction of *Harry Potter*, for instance, retold the narrative as if Harry Potter was a transwoman instead, as a way of rebelling against J. K. Rowling's transphobic comments and views.

Cosplay, similarly, allows fans to take ownership over aspects of the narrative and retell it in ways they prefer. This can involve reimagining themselves in the place of the character, or sometimes creating an entirely new character simply set in the world. In other instances, they alter the gender of the character either by changing the costume or by donning the costume on their own other-gendered body. Cosplay is, however, far more easily viewable than fanfiction. It does not require going to specific websites. Cosplay pops up easily on social media feeds, showing us the alterations and fan control through an easy-to-view image the viewer can click on or readily share.

Fans who cosplay, therefore, are in a complex relationship with the pieces of popular culture they are adorning themselves with. They initially choose their character from a work they feel a connection to, but it is a specific type of connection. What this connection feels like can vary, but it ranges from a massive interest in the franchise generally to a deep empathetic understanding of one particular character. If the cosplayer is crafting the costume, the process of making the costume can help to restate to the cosplayer their emotional connections.

But the donning of the costume is not simply the fiction acting on the cosplayer. In the choice of character, we see how cosplayers are initially drawn to their fictions and how these fictions become increasingly interesting by being inscribed on the cosplayer's body. The cosplayer, however, has an active role in this process. By donning the costume and performing that identity, the cosplayer is, in turn, acting back on to the fiction itself. This is all due to the joint performance of both the character and the cosplayer.

In cosplay, there is a negotiation which occurs, one distinctive to each individual cosplay, not just to each cosplayer. The result of this negotiation is, in many ways, a direct acting on the performance of the fiction. The character is transformed simply through the act of cosplaying. It's not just that Sam is pretending to be Tohru Honda temporarily – it is that in this moment of time there is a form of Tohru Honda unique to Sam and their performance. It is not just someone being Tohru, which can be replaced with anyone else's cosplay of the same character. The unique quality of Sam's performance is understood by both the cosplayer and the viewer.

Similarly, cosplay can also impact how the cosplayer understands their own body and the relationship the cosplayer has with their body. Micah, a non-binary cosplayer, talked about how their play with costume and identity performance led them to realize their own gender identity. This was also reflected in Arthur, a transman. Arthur talked about how their start with cosplay coincided with their own gender realization, as well as around the time of puberty, describing the time as a 'big jumbling mess'. Cosplay helped them to play with gender binaries and the performed identity of gender, in order to come to a greater understanding of themself: 'Through cosplay, I'm able to explore that and explore femininity and masculinity and enjoy . . . androgynous-ness.'

We started this book by exploring how popular culture is our contemporary mythology, and how the performance of cosplay is somewhat akin to mythic performance. As we've looked at the complicatedly beautiful world of cosplay, we've also seen just how deeply interesting cosplay performance can be. We have reflected on how cosplayers are able to actively change aspects of the original media form through their performance. In this chapter, we've flipped the script, seeing how the art of cosplay impacts the lives of cosplayers. This is because mythology, and storytelling more generally, are rarely a one-way street. As much as we have power over the way we tell our stories, as Seth Kunin likes to remind us, we are also impacted by the power the stories have over us.[8] We started with a reminder of what a myth is – a story someone uses to understand themself and the world around us. While I, at first, demonstrated this through the way people talk about the fictions they love, we can now think about what this means for cosplayers more fully.

Obviously, when they pick their fiction to cosplay, this is because of that initial love of the fiction. For Sam, for example, they picked Tohru Honda because of their love and connection to the story as it was. They saw themself somewhere in it. But then they wore the costume, and in the process they were able to feel a little of that narrative power, transforming the way they thought of themself in relation to their own grief. For Emma and Riley, their connection to story came first, but through cosplaying they came to understand themselves and their skin tone in a more self-compassionate way, while still reflecting on the issues present in racial representation in pop culture more generally.

In each of these examples, the myth comes first. But the performance of the myth – the cosplay of the myth – is what allows the individual cosplayers to see themselves in a different light. They are able to feel more confident in themselves, in their bodies and in their social worlds. Elliot and Adrian both reflected on the utter joy of just putting on a costume to go to the local coffee shop. Riley reflected on the passion put into creating costumes and the confidence that comes with wearing them. Blake talked about the power of cosplay in identity transformation, and how they not only act different but *feel* different in different costumes.

There are two fascinating aspects when doing research like this and talking to so many different people from different backgrounds, even living in different countries. The first is when cosplayers inherently disagree. I can ask the same question to twenty different cosplayers and get twenty different answers. We saw how contentious some issues can be, as with 'sexy' cosplays, or 'lewd' cosplays as Sam put it. But the other interesting thing is when you ask the twenty different cosplayers from twenty different backgrounds the same question and you get the exact same answer. When it came to feeling impacted by their costume, feeling comfortable in the self during the cosplay, this is what united all the cosplayers I spoke to. Every one of them talked about how important cosplay is to their life and how it makes them feel more like themself, even when acting as a different person. When talking to me about this, Emma became very nervous and kept explaining that they know it 'sounds crazy'. When I told them I had heard the same thing over and over again, they lit up and said, 'Of course!'

What makes cosplay inherently important to every single cosplayer is not just the art form, though that remains important for some. It's not the skill involved in costume construction, though that remains important for some. It's not the fun in performing as

Cosplayers at MegaCon Manchester 2022.

the character at cons, though that remains important for some. What united all cosplayers, what made it important for every single one of them, was that they understood the reciprocal relationship storytelling had with their identity. Not only did fiction impact them personally, but they could impact it right back.

There is a power in cosplay, one where the cosplayer is not passive in relation to the media they are consuming but actively changing and altering narratives in their own performance. Their stories are also being told along with the stories from the original media. Cosplayers have a voice, a loud voice, that can be present alongside the original narrative, not behind it.

And the impact of the cosplayers' narrative, the knowledge of their innate power that is present every time they put on a costume, transforms their sense of self. They gain confidence. Sometimes, this confidence is bodily, as in the case of those who reported often being less confident in the look of their body. But it can also be confidence in self. They gain confidence in who they are as a person, or more collectively who they are as a community.

As we stated at the very beginning of this book, cosplay is a lot more than just 'dressing up'. It's an inherent connection to narrative, one that shows how individuals are able to use fiction as a way to solidify or identify themselves and their own ways of viewing the world. Cosplay is an important part of the complicated history of the art of dressing, one which builds on the long history of masquerades, masks and fashion. It's a performance where cosplayers pose, dance and speak as the characters, but also flow out of the performance to be themselves fluidly and as it suits them. Cosplay may not be rooted to place, but it takes inspiration from the places it thrives in. It's a connection to community, to like-minded individuals who love to create and who love fiction in the same way they do. It's a way to show off and hone skill that is physical as well as emotional or intellectual. It has an impact on our understanding of gender and of sexuality. But it's a form of dressing that cosplayers have control over, one which they can transform at will to suit their personal needs or – more importantly – their personal identities. It allows cosplayers to demonstrate needs in our popular culture media, like diverse representation. It gives cosplayers confidence to be themselves, and to love the cultural narratives we love without shame, without apology and with each other.

Cosplay is not just dressing up, but a powerful, skilful art which demonstrates the importance of popular culture narratives. But more importantly, it also demonstrates the value of the individual, the fan, who grabs hold of what they love and will not rest until they have left their mark on the world.

REFERENCES

1 Myth, Pop Culture and Cosplay

1 Edward Burnett Tylor, *Primitive Culture: Researches into the Development of Mythology, Philosophy, Religion, Art, and Custom* (Cambridge, 2010).
2 William Bascom, 'The Forms of Folklore: Prose Narratives', in *Sacred Narrative: Readings in the Theory of Myth*, ed. Alan Dundes (Berkeley, CA, 1984), pp. 5–29.
3 Joseph Campbell, *The Hero with a Thousand Faces* (New York, 1997), for example. Problems with conceptions of myth as metaphor can be explored in Amba Sepie, 'More than Stories, More than Myths: Animal/Human/Nature(s) in Traditional Ecological Worldviews', *Humanities*, VI/4 (2017).
4 Seth Kunin, *The Logic of Incest: A Structuralist Analysis of Hebrew Mythology* (Sheffield, 1995); Vivian Asimos, *Digital Mythology and the Internet's Monster* (London, 2021).
5 Joseph Laycock, 'Myth Sells: Mattel's Commission of The Masters of the Universe Bible', *Journal of Religion and Popular Culture*, XXII/2 (2010), p. 4.
6 Michel de Certeau, *The Practice of Everyday Life*, trans. Stephen Rendall (Berkeley, CA, 2013).
7 Ibid., p. 174.
8 Henry Jenkins, *Textual Poachers: Television Fans and Participatory Culture* (New York, 1992).
9 Cornel Sandvoss, *Fans: The Mirror of Consumption* (Cambridge, 2005), p. 8.

2 The Art of Dressing

1 Timothy A. Unwin, *Jules Verne: Journeys in Writing* (Liverpool, 2005).
2 Holly Swinyard, *A Guide to Film and TV Cosplay* (Barnsley, 2021).
3 Malcolm Barnard, 'Introduction', in *Fashion as Communication*, ed. Malcolm Barnard (London, 2008), pp. 1–7.

4 Joanne Entwistle, 'Fashion and the Fleshy Body: Dress as Embodied Practice', *Fashion Theory*, IV/3 (2000), pp. 323–47.

5 Mary Douglas, *Natural Symbols: Explorations in Cosmology* (New York, 2003).

6 Maurice Merleau-Ponty, *The Primacy of Perception: And Other Essays on Phenomenological Psychology, the Philosophy of Art, History, and Politics*, trans. William Cobb (Evanston, IL, 1976), p. 5.

7 Erving Goffman, *Presentation of Self in Everyday Life* (London, 2007).

8 Fred Davis, *Fashion, Culture, and Identity* (Chicago, 2008), p. 25.

9 See, for example, Dick Hebdige, 'Subculture and Style', in *The Consumption Reader*, ed. David B. Clarke, Marcus A. Doel and Kate M. L. Housiaux (London, 2003); Therèsa M. Winge, *Body Style* (London, 2012).

10 Amy Milligan, 'American Bodylore and Folk Dress', in *The Oxford Handbook of American Folklore and Folklife Studies*, ed. Simon J. Bronner (New York, 2018), pp. 452–69.

11 Katharine Galloway Young, 'Introduction', in *Bodylore*, ed. Katharine Galloway Young (Knoxville, TN, 1995), pp. xvii–xxiv.

12 Matthew Hale, 'Cosplay: Intertextuality, Public Texts, and the Body Fantastic', *Western Folklore*, LXXIII/1 (2014), pp. 5–37.

13 Catherine Bell, 'The Ritual Body and the Dynamics of Ritual Power', *Journal of Ritual Studies*, IV/2 (1990), pp. 299–313.

14 John Emigh, *Masked Performance: The Play of Self and Other in Ritual and Theatre* (Philadelphia, PA, 1996).

3 Cosplay and the Art of Performance

1 Joel Gn, 'Queer Simulation: The Practice, Performance and Pleasure of Cosplay', *Continuum*, XXV/4 (2011), pp. 583–93.

2 Richard Schechner, *Performance Studies: An Introduction* (London, 2002).

3 Seth Kunin describes this in greater detail (Seth D. Kunin, 'Juggling Identities among the Crypto-Jews of the American Southwest', *Religion*, XXXI/1 (2001), pp. 41–61), primarily focused on how individuals juggle multiple narratives in a process he calls 'jonglerie'. The connection between cosplay and jonglerie will be discussed more in Chapter Seven.

4 A. David Napier, *Masks, Transformation, and Paradox* (Berkeley, CA, 1986). See also John Emigh, *Masked Performance: The Play of Self and Other in Ritual and Theatre* (Philadelphia, PA, 1996).

5 Claude Lévi-Strauss, *The Naked Man*, trans. John Weightman and Doreen Weightman (London, 1981), pp. 669–71.

6 Jacques Galinier, 'A Lévi-Straussian Controversy Revisited: The Implicit Mythology of Rituals in a Mesoamerican Context', *Journal of the Southwest*, XLVI/4 (2004), pp. 661–77.

7 Jonathan Miles-Watson, 'The Cathedral on the Ridge and the Implicit Mythology of the Shimla Hills', *Suomen Antropologi: Journal of the Finnish Anthropological Society*, XXXVII/4 (2012), pp. 30–46.
8 Jay Mechling, 'Picturing Hunting', *Western Folklore*, LXIII/1–2 (2004), pp. 51–78.
9 Richard Chalfen, 'Introduction to the Study of Non-Professional Photography as Visual Communication', in *Saying Cheese: Studies in Folklore and Visual Communication*, ed. Stephen Ohrn and Michael Bell, Folklore Forum No. 13 (Bloomington, IN, 1975), pp. 19–25.
10 Richard Chalfen, *Turning Leaves: The Photograph Collections of Two Japanese American Families* (Albuquerque, NM, 1991).

4 Cosplaying in Place

1 Theresa Winge, 'Costuming the Imagination: Origins of Anime and Manga Cosplay', *Mechademia*, I (2006), pp. 65–76.
2 See Chapter Two; also Timothy A. Unwin, *Jules Verne: Journeys in Writing* (Liverpool, 2005).
3 Stijn Reijnders, *Places of the Imagination: Media, Tourism, Culture* (Farnham, 2011).
4 Nicolle Lamerichs, 'Costuming as Subculture: The Multiple Bodies of Cosplay', *Scene*, II/1 (2014), pp. 113–25.
5 Vivian Asimos, 'Navigating through Space Butterflies: CoxCon 2017 and Fieldwork Presentation of Contemporary Movements', *Fieldwork in Religion*, XIV/2 (2019), pp. 181–94.
6 Benedict Anderson, *Imagined Communities: Reflections on the Origin and Spread of Nationalism* (London, 1983).

5 Cosplay's Community

1 Dick Hebdige, 'Subculture and Style', in *The Consumption Reader*, ed. David B. Clarke, Marcus A. Doel and Kate M. L. Housiaux (London and New York, 2003), pp. 150–51.
2 Ibid.
3 Michel Maffesoli, *The Time of the Tribes: The Decline of Individualism in Mass Society* (London, 1996).
4 Anne Hardy, Andy Bennett and Brady Robards, eds, *Neo-Tribes: Consumption, Leisure and Tourism* (Cham, 2018).
5 Albert O. Hirschman, *Shifting Involvements: Private Interest and Public Action* (Princeton, NJ, and Oxford, 2002).
6 Benedict Anderson, *Imagined Communities: Reflections on the Origin and Spread of Nationalism* (London, 1983).

6 Skill and Cosplay

1 Gísli Pálsson, 'Enskilment at Sea', *Man*, new series, XXIX/4 (1994), pp. 901–27.
2 Erving Goffman, *The Presentation of Self in Everyday Life* [1956] (London, 2007).
3 Umberto Eco, 'Lumbar Thought', in *Travels in Hyper-Reality: Essays* (San Diego, CA, 1990).

7 Cosplay, Gender and Sexuality

1 Incidental Mythology, 'Fandom and Cosplay (feat. Holly Swinyard)', *The Religion and Popular Culture Podcast*, Season 3, Episode 11 (2022), www.incidentalmythology.com.
2 Elizabeth Wilson, *Adorned in Dreams: Fashion and Modernity*, rev. edn (London, 2013).
3 Joanne Entwistle, 'Fashion and the Fleshy Body: Dress as Embodied Practice', *Fashion Theory*, IV/3 (2000), pp. 323–47.
4 Judith Butler, 'Critically Queer', *GLQ*, I (1993), pp. 17–32; p. 21.
5 Harry Barbee and Douglas Schrock, 'Un/Gendering Social Selves: How Nonbinary People Navigate and Experience a Binarily Gendered World', *Sociological Forum*, XXXIV/3 (2019), pp. 572–93.

8 The Transformative Art of Cosplay

1 Seth D. Kunin, 'Juggling Identities among the Crypto-Jews of the American Southwest', *Religion*, XXXI/1 (2001), pp. 41–61.
2 Michel de Certeau, *The Practice of Everyday Life* (Berkeley, CA, 2013); Henry Jenkins, *Textual Poachers: Television Fans and Participatory Culture* (New York, 1992).
3 Abby Day, *Believing in Belonging: Belief and Social Identity in the Modern World* (Oxford, 2011).
4 Richard Schechner, *Performance Studies: An Introduction* (London, 2002).
5 Jane McGonigal, 'A Real Little Game: The Performance of Belief in Pervasive Play', *Proceedings of DiGRA 2003* (2003).
6 Michael Kinsella, *Legend-Tripping Online: Supernatural Folklore and the Search for Ong's Hat* (Jackson, MS, 2011).
7 Linda Dégh and Andrew Vázsonyi, 'Does the Word "Dog" Bite? Ostensive Action: A Means of Legend-Telling', *Journal of Folklore Research*, XX/1 (1983), pp. 5–34.
8 Vivian Asimos, 'Everything Is True Here, Even If It Isn't: The Performance of Belief Online', *Journal of the British Association for the Study of Religion*, XXII (2020), pp. 44–54.

9 Kinsella, *Legend-Tripping Online*, p. 5.
10 Claude Lévi-Strauss, 'The Effectiveness of Symbols', in *Structural Anthropology*, trans. C. Jacobson and B. G. Schoepf (New York, 1963), pp. 186–205.
11 Victor Turner, *The Ritual Process: Structure and Anti-Structure* (New York, 1969).
12 Judith Butler, *Bodies that Matter: On the Discursive Limits of 'Sex'* (New York, 1993).

9 Storytelling with Body and Identity

1 May Douglas, *Natural Symbols: Explorations in Cosmology* (New York, 2003), pp. 72–91.
2 Judith Butler, *Bodies that Matter: On the Discursive Limits of 'Sex'* (New York, 1993).
3 Daniel Ben-Amos, 'The Idea of Folklore: An Essay', in *Studies in Aggadah and Jewish Folklore*, ed. Issachar Ben-Ami and Joseph Dan (Jerusalem, 1983), pp. 11–17.
4 Erving Goffman, *The Presentation of Self in Everyday Life* [1956] (London, 2007).
5 Incidental Mythology, 'Fandom and Cosplay (feat. Holly Swinyard)', *The Religion and Popular Culture Podcast*, Season 3, Episode 11 (2022), www.incidentalmythology.com.
6 Mat Hames, dir., *Becoming Jessica Nigri* (2018).
7 Henry Jenkins, *Textual Poachers: Television Fans and Participatory Culture* (New York, 1992).
8 Seth D. Kunin, 'Juggling Identities among the Crypto-Jews of the American Southwest', *Religion*, XXXI/1 (2001), pp. 41–61.

BIBLIOGRAPHY

Anderson, Benedict, *Imagined Communities: Reflections on the Origin and Spread of Nationalism* (London, 1983)

Arnold, Rebecca, *Fashion: A Very Short Introduction* (New York, 2009)

Asimos, Vivian, *Digital Mythology and the Internet's Monster* (London, 2021)

——, 'Everything Is True Here, Even If It Isn't: The Performance of Belief Online', *Journal of the British Association for the Study of Religion*, XXII (2020), pp. 44–54

——, 'Navigating through Space Butterflies: CoxCon 2017 and Fieldwork Presentation of Contemporary Movements', *Fieldwork in Religion*, XIV/2 (2019), pp. 181–94

Barbee, Harry, and Douglas Schrock, 'Un/Gendering Social Selves: How Nonbinary People Navigate and Experience a Binarily Gendered World', *Sociological Forum*, XXXIV/3 (2019), pp. 572–93

Barbieri, Donatella, *Costume in Performance: Materiality, Culture, and the Body* (London, 2017)

Barnard, Malcolm, 'Introduction', in *Fashion as Communication*, ed. Malcolm Barnard (London, 2008), pp. 1–7

Bascom, William, 'The Forms of Folklore: Prose Narratives', in *Sacred Narrative: Readings in the Theory of Myth*, ed. Alan Dundes (Berkeley, CA, 1984), pp. 5–29

Bell, Catherine, 'The Ritual Body and the Dynamics of Ritual Power', *Journal of Ritual Studies*, IV/2 (1990), pp. 299–313

Ben-Amos, Dan, 'The Idea of Folklore: An Essay', in *Studies in Aggadah and Jewish Folklore*, ed. Issachar Ben-Ami and Joseph Dan (Jerusalem, 1983), pp. 11–17

Bobel, Chris, and Samantha Kwan, eds, *Embodied Resistance: Challenging the Norms, Breaking the Rules* (Nashville, TN, 2011)

Booth, Paul, ed., *A Companion to Media Fandom and Fan Studies* (Hoboken, NJ, 2018)

Butler, Judith, *Bodies that Matter: On the Discursive Limits of 'Sex'* (New York, 1993)
——, 'Critically Queer', GLQ, I (1993), pp. 17–32
Campbell, Joseph, *The Hero with a Thousand Faces* (New York, 1997)
Certeau, Michel de, *The Practice of Everyday Life* (Berkeley, CA, 2013)
Chalfen, Richard, 'Introduction to the Study of Non-Professional Photography as Visual Communication', in *Saying Cheese: Studies in Folklore and Visual Communication*, ed. Stephen Ohrn and Michael Bell (Bloomington, IN, 1975), pp. 19–25
——, *Turning Leaves: The Photograph Collections of Two Japanese American Families* (Albuquerque, NM, 1991)
Crawford, Garry, and David Hancock, *Cosplay and the Art of Play: Exploring Sub-Culture Through Art* (Cham, 2019)
Davis, Fred, *Fashion, Culture, and Identity* (Chicago, 2008)
Day, Abby, *Believing in Belonging: Belief and Social Identity in the Modern World* (Oxford, 2011)
Dégh, Linda, and Andrew Vázsonyi, 'Does the Word "Dog" Bite? Ostensive Action: A Means of Legend-Telling', *Journal of Folklore Research*, XX/1 (1983), pp. 5–34
Douglas, Mary, *Natural Symbols: Explorations in Cosmology* (New York, 2003)
Eco, Umberto, 'Lumbar Thought', in *Travels in Hyper-Reality: Essays* (San Diego, CA, 1990)
Emigh, John, *Masked Performance: The Play of Self and Other in Ritual and Theatre* (Philadelphia, PA, 1996)
Entwistle, Joanne, 'Fashion and the Fleshy Body: Dress as Embodied Practice', *Fashion Theory*, IV/3 (2000), pp. 323–47
Featherstone, Mike, and Bryan S. Turner, 'Body and Society: An Introduction', *Body and Society*, I/1 (1995), pp. 1–12
Galinier, Jacques, 'A Lévi-Straussian Controversy Revisited: The Implicit Mythology of Rituals in a Mesoamerican Context', *Journal of the Southwest*, XLVI/4 (2004), pp. 661–77
Gn, Joel, 'Queer Simulation: The Practice, Performance and Pleasure of Cosplay', *Continuum*, XXV/4 (2011), pp. 583–93
Goffman, Erving, *The Presentation of Self in Everyday Life* (London, 2007)
Hale, Matthew, 'Cosplay: Intertextuality, Public Texts, and the Body Fantastic', *Western Folklore*, LXXIII/1 (2014), pp. 5–37
Hames, Mat, dir., *Becoming Jessica Nigri* (2018)
Hardy, Anne, Andy Bennett and Brady Robards, eds, *Neo-Tribes: Consumption, Leisure and Tourism* (Cham, 2018)
Hebdige, Dick, 'Subculture and Style', in *The Consumption Reader*, ed. David B. Clarke, Marcus A. Doel and Kate M. L. Housiaux (London, 2003), pp. 150–51

Hirschman, Albert O., *Shifting Involvements: Private Interest and Public Action* (Princeton, NJ, and Oxford, 2002)

Incidental Mythology, 'Fandom and Cosplay (feat. Holly Swinyard)', *The Religion and Popular Culture Podcast*, Season 3, Episode 11 (2022), www.incidentalmythology.com

Jenkins, Henry, *Textual Poachers: Television Fans and Participatory Culture* (New York, 1992)

Kinsella, Michael, *Legend-Tripping Online: Supernatural Folklore and the Search for Ong's Hat* (Jackson, MS, 2011)

Kunin, Seth D., 'Juggling Identities among the Crypto-Jews of the American Southwest', *Religion*, XXXI/1 (2001), pp. 41–61

——, *The Logic of Incest: A Structuralist Analysis of Hebrew Mythology* (Sheffield, 1995)

Lamerichs, Nicolle, 'Costuming as Subculture: The Multiple Bodies of Cosplay', *Scene*, II/1 (2014), pp. 113–25

——, *Productive Fandom: Intermediality and Affective Reception in Fan Cultures* (Amsterdam, 2018)

——, 'Stranger than Fiction: Fan Identity in Cosplay', *Transformative Works and Cultures*, VII (2011)

Laycock, Joseph, 'Myth Sells: Mattel's Commission of The Masters of the Universe Bible', *Journal of Religion and Popular Culture*, XXII/2 (2010), p. 4

Lévi-Strauss, Claude, 'The Effectiveness of Symbols', in *Structural Anthropology*, trans. C. Jacobson and B. G. Schoepf (New York, 1963), pp. 186–205

——, *The Naked Man*, trans. John Weightman and Doreen Weightman (London, 1981)

McGonigal, Jane, 'A Real Little Game: The Performance of Belief in Pervasive Play', *Proceedings of DiGRA 2003* (2003)

Maffesoli, Michel, *The Time of the Tribes: The Decline of Individualism in Mass Society*, Theory, Culture and Society (London, 1996)

Mechling, Jay, 'Picturing Hunting', *Western Folklore*, LXIII/1–2 (2004), pp. 51–78

Merleau-Ponty, Maurice, *The Primacy of Perception: And Other Essays on Phenomenological Psychology, the Philosophy of Art, History, and Politics*, trans. William Cobb [1964] (Evanston, IL, 1976)

Miles-Watson, Jonathan, 'The Cathedral on the Ridge and the Implicit Mythology of the Shimla Hills', *Suomen Antropologi: Journal of the Finnish Anthropological Society*, XXXVII/4 (2012), pp. 30–46

Milligan, Amy, 'American Bodylore and Folk Dress', in *The Oxford Handbook of American Folklore and Folklife Studies*, ed. Simon J. Bronner (New York, 2018), pp. 452–69

Mountfort, Paul, Anne Peirson-Smith and Adam Geczy, *Planet Cosplay: Costume Play, Identity and Global Fandom* (Bristol, 2019)

Napier, A. David, *Masks, Transformation, and Paradox* (Berkeley, CA, 1986)

Pálsson, Gísli, 'Enskilment at Sea', *Man*, new series, XXIX/4 (1994), pp. 901–27

Rahman, Osmud, Liu Wing-Sun and Brittany Hei-man Cheung, '"Cosplay": Imaginative Self and Performing Identity', *Fashion Theory: The Journal of Dress, Body and Culture*, XVI/3 (2012), pp. 317–41

Reijnders, Stijn, *Places of the Imagination: Media, Tourism, Culture* (Farnham, 2011)

Sandvoss, Cornel, *Fans: The Mirror of Consumption* (Cambridge, 2005)

Schechner, Richard, *Performance Studies: An Introduction* (London, 2002)

Sepie, Amba, 'More than Stories, More than Myths: Animal/Human/Nature(s) in Traditional Ecological Worldviews', *Humanities*, VI/4 (2017).

Swinyard, Holly, *A Guide to Film and TV Cosplay* (Barnsley, 2021)

Turner, Victor, *The Ritual Process: Structure and Anti-Structure* (New York, 1969)

Tylor, Edward Burnett, *Primitive Culture: Researches into the Development of Mythology, Philosophy, Religion, Art, and Custom* (Cambridge, 2010)

Unwin, Timothy A., *Jules Verne: Journeys in Writing* (Liverpool, 2005)

Wilson, Elizabeth, *Adorned in Dreams: Fashion and Modernity*, rev. edn (London, 2013)

Winge, Therèsa M., *Body Style* (London, 2012)

——, 'Costuming the Imagination: Origins of Anime and Manga Cosplay', *Mechademia*, I (2006), pp. 65–76

Young, Katharine Galloway, 'Introduction', in *Bodylore*, ed. Katharine Galloway Young (Knoxville, TN, 1995), pp. xvii–xxiv

——, 'Whose Body? An Introduction to Bodylore', *Journal of American Folklore*, CVII/423 (1994), pp. 3–8

ACKNOWLEDGEMENTS

First, I want to thank every single cosplayer who agreed to interviews and who chatted to me during cons or photoshoots; the cosplay photographers who generously agreed for their images to appear in this text; and everyone who so wonderfully gave their time to reflect on this work. Without you and your experiences, this book would not exist.

A special thanks also goes to my wonderful and understanding husband, Tom. You're always so understanding of late-night to-do lists, and how I let my work and books take over my life. I love you so very much, and am so grateful for your presence in my life.

And of course, a wonderful thanks goes to my backers on Indiegogo, without whom I would have been unable to even start to do some of the research featured in this book, most notably: Stacia Asimos, William Leung, Robyn Mellish, Emma Asimos, Tom Asimos, Macie Jones, James Murphy, Ben Wicks, Jennifer Uzzell, Phyllis Wicks, Jeremy Bear, Stephen Jacobs and Theodora Wildcroft. Thank you from the bottom of my heart.

PHOTO
ACKNOWLEDGEMENTS

The author and publishers wish to express their thanks to the sources listed below for illustrative material and/or permission to reproduce it:

Photos Megaera Amis, *Cosplay Journal*: pp. 129, 143, 144; photos Vivian Asimos: pp. 53, 64, 73, 74, 77, 81, 83, 84, 85, 92, 106, 116, 122, 126, 127, 135, 149, 157, 158, 171; photos Nigel Hart, Cosplay Academy: pp. 132, 139; photos SonSon Photography: pp. 131, 141; from *Tacoma Times*, IX/133 (24 May 1912), photo Washington State Library, Olympia: p. 36; photos Thomas Wicks: pp. 31, 51, 69, 130, 133, 134, 136, 137, 138, 140, 142, 212.

INDEX